Laboratory Atlas
of Anatomy
and Physiology

SECOND EDITION

Douglas J. Eder, PhD
Southern Illinois University—Edwardsville

Shari Lewis Kaminsky, DPM

John W. Bertram

WCB
McGraw-Hill

Boston, Massachusetts   Burr Ridge, Illinois   Dubuque, Iowa
Madison, Wisconsin   New York, New York   San Francisco, California   St. Louis, Missouri

McGraw-Hill
A Division of the McGraw-Hill Companies

LABORATORY ATLAS OF ANATOMY AND PHYSIOLOGY

1 2 3 4 5 6 7 8 9 0 QPD/QPD 9 0 9 8 7

ISBN 0–697–39480–8

Publisher: *Kevin T. Kane/Michael D. Lange*

Sponsoring Editor: *Kristine Noel Tibbetts*

Developmental Editor: *Brittany Rossman*

Marketing Manager: *Keri Witman*

Project Manager: *Jane C. Morgan*

Production Supervisor: *Deb Donner*

Interior design: *Barb Hodgson*

Photo research coordinator: *Lori Hancock*

Compositor: *Interactive Composition Corporation*

Typeface: *10/12 Goudy*

Printer: *Quebecor Printing Book Group/Dubuque*

Credits: Chapter 1: All photos by Ed Reschke except figures 1–89 and 1–90
    Chapters 2 and 4: Douglas Eder, Shari Lewis Kaminsky, and John Bertram
    Chapter 3: The following figures were taken from Shier/Butler/Lewis, *Hole's Human Anatomy & Physiology*, 7th Edition: 3.1, 3.2, 3.6, 3.7, 3.10, 3.11, 3.13, 3.14, 3.15, 3.16, 3.17, 3.18, 3.19, 3.20, 3.21, 3.22, 3.23. The following figures were taken from Van De Graaff/Fox *Human Anatomy & Physiology*, 4th Edition: 3.5, 3.8, 3.9. The following figures were taken from Seeley/Stephens/Tate, *Anatomy & Physiology*, 4th Edition: 3.3, 3.4
    Chapter 5: Table 5.29 contains material adapted from Van De Graaff/Fox *Concepts of Human Anatomy & Physiology*, 4th Edition.

CONTENTS

DEDICATION

To our spouses
Suzanne, Joe, and Mary Ellen

ACKNOWLEDGMENTS

We obtained all animal material pictured from Nasco Company, Ft. Atkinson, Wisconsin. Cat cadavers were skinned at the factory and packed in a non-formaldehyde preservative. At our request, Nasco personnel selected particularly well-injected cadavers for us; we thank them for this service. We would also like to thank our colleague, Dave Bolt of West Hills College, who reviewed our animal dissections.

Histology

Simple Cuboidal Epithelium

Figure 1-1
Interphase   Nuclear membrane intact with chromatin visible. (×250)

Chromatin
Nuclear membrane

Figure 1-2
Prophase   Duplicated chromosomes condensed into visible strands; nuclear membrane absent. (×250)

Chromosome

Figure 1-3
Metaphase   Darkly stained chromosomes positioned by microtubular framework to align at cell equator. Spindle fibers and aster visible. (×250)

Chromosomes
Spindle fibers
Aster

Figure 1-4
Anaphase   Darkly stained chromosomes move to opposite poles under microtubular influence. Spindle fibers and aster visible. (×250)

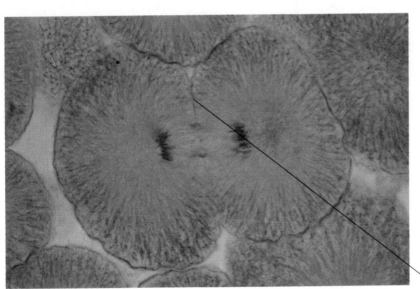

Cleavage furrow at equator

Figure 1-5
Telophase   Separated chromosomes lose microtubular attachments. Belt of actinomyocin forms at equator, assists in formation of new cell membranes and cytokinesis. Cleavage furrow forms two daughter cells. (×250)

Figure 1-6
Simple Squamous Epithelium   Single layer
of flat cells covering a surface. From human
omentum. (×250)

Fixed macrophage

Simple squamous epithelium

Nucleus

Basement membrane

Figure 1-7
Simple Squamous Epithelium   Surface view
of flattened cells. Human mesothelium.
(×250)

Nucleus

Figure 1-8
Simple Cuboidal Epithelium   Although
not strictly cube shaped, cuboidal cells are
roughly equidimensional in length, width,
and depth. Single layer of cells lining
surface of kidney tubules. Cross section.
(×250)

Simple cuboidal epithelium

Lumen of tubule

Basement membrane

Figure 1-9
Simple Cuboidal Epithelium Longitudinal section of kidney tubule. (×250)

Basement membrane

Simple cuboidal epithelium

Lumen of tubule

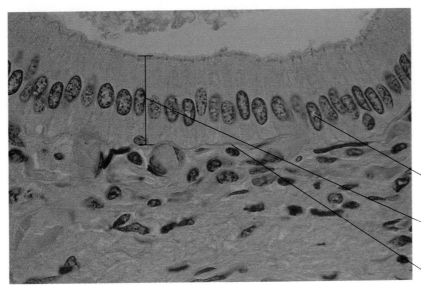

Figure 1-10
Simple Columnar Epithelium Cellular height is much greater than width or length. Nuclei generally appear in a row. From pancreatic duct. (×250)

Nucleus

Simple columnar epithelium

Basement membrane

Figure 1-11
Pseudostratified Ciliated Columnar Epithelium Nuclei appear to lie in two rows, but in fact all cells in single layer are in contact with basement membrane. Section shows well-defined cilia, three goblet cells, basement membrane, underlying connective tissue. From monkey trachea. (×100)

Nucleus

Cilia

Goblet cell

Basement membrane

Figure 1-12

Pseudostratified Ciliated Columnar Epithelium   Section shows cilia, multiple layers of nuclei, basement membrane, underlying connective tissue. From human trachea. (×250)

Cilia

Basement membrane

Nucleus

Figure 1-13

Stratified Squamous Epithelium   Flattened cells at surface change to less flattened morphology in deeper layers. Oral cavity of rabbit. (×100)

Figure 1-14
Stratified Squamous Epithelium   Flattened, keratinized cells at surface show variations in form in deeper layers. From papilla in human skin. (×100)

Keratinized cells

Figure 1-15
Transitional Epithelium from Urinary Bladder   Umbrella cells stretch and flatten as bladder fills. Basement membrane separates epithelium from underlying connective tissue containing blood vessels. (×250)

Umbrella cell

Basement membrane

Blood vessel lumen

Figure 1-16
Dense Regular Elastic Tissue   Extracellular elastin fibers running parallel in a plane. Structure permits tissue elasticity and recoil. From aorta. (×100)

Elastin fiber

Figure 1-17
Reticular Connective Tissue   Mesh of reticular fibers appears as dark lines; provides scaffold for cellular organization of this lymph node. (×250)

Reticular fiber

Figure 1-18
Loose (Areolar) Fibrous Connective Tissue Pink bands of collagen run in all directions through intercellular spaces of subcutaneous tissue, permit flexible resistance to mechanical stress. (×100)

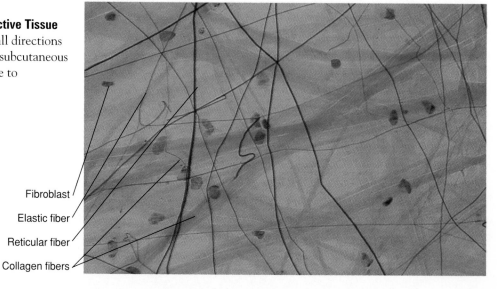

Fibroblast

Elastic fiber

Reticular fiber

Collagen fibers

Figure 1-19

Dense Fibrous Connective Tissue   Bands of collagen running in regular, parallel rows resist mechanical stress mainly along course of fibers. Monkey tendon. (×250)

Collagen fibers

Nucleus of fibroblast

Figure 1-20

Dense Fibrous Connective Tissue   Bands of collagen running in irregular rows give multidirectional tensile strength. Collagen-secreting fibroblasts appear throughout. From aponeurosis. (×100)

Nuclei of fibroblasts

Collagen fibers

Figure 1-21

Adipose Tissue   Large, empty, polyhedral vacuoles dominate small, eccentrically located cell nuclei of adipocytes. Fine capillaries run through tissue. (×100)

Vacuole

Nucleus

Capillary

Figure 1-22

Fibrocartilage   Cell nests of chondrocytes in territorial matrix surrounded by coarse extracellular fibers. (×250)

Chondrocyte

Figure 1-23

Hyaline Cartilage   During interstitial growth, cartilage cells often form small clusters and move apart as they secrete extracellular matrix. (×100)

Chondrocytes

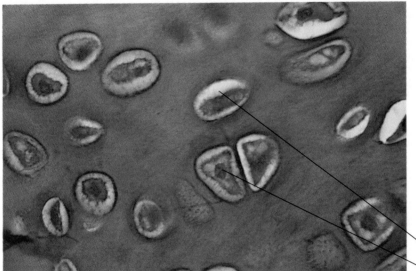

Figure 1-24
Hyaline Cartilage   Artifactual vacuolation forms characteristic lacuna around chondrocyte cell bodies. From trachea. (×250)

Lacuna

Chondrocyte

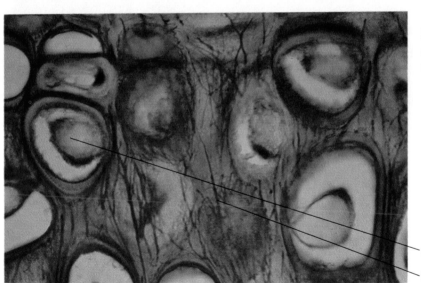

Figure 1-25
Elastic Cartilage   Extracellular matrix contains elastic fibers that confer elastic recoil to this tissue. (×250)

Chondrocyte

Elastin fiber

Figure 1-26

Skin   Thick, keratinized, multilayered **stratum corneum** rests atop grainy **stratum granulosum** (stratum lucidum not clearly evident). **Stratum spinosum,** composed of irregularly shaped cells with indistinct nuclei, lies atop single, clearly nucleated **stratum basale**. Human palm. (×100)

Stratum corneum

Stratum granulosum

Stratum spinosum

Stratum basale

Figure 1-27

Skin   Squamous epidermis with cornified layers overlying darkly stained stratum basale and connective tissue of underlying dermis. Single papilla visible. Human scalp. (×100)

Papilla

Epidermis

Dermis

Figure 1-28

Meissner's Corpuscle in Dermis   Elongated oval body located in dermis just below stratum basale is thought to be responsible for part of fine touch reception. (×100)

Meissner's corpuscle

Figure 1-29
Pacinian Corpuscle   Encapsulated nerve ending found deep in dermis and throughout interior of body detects pressure. (×25)

Free nerve ending

Figure 1-30
Human Scalp with Hair Follicle   Follicle root, with sheath embedded in pale adipose tissue, has sebaceous glands surrounding it near surface. (×10)

Hair follicle
Sebaceous gland

Figure 1-31
Detail of Sebaceous Gland   Nucleated germinative cells at base of gland mature and accumulate lipid. At duct, they degenerate and lyse to release their oily product, sebum. (×100)

Sebaceous gland
Hair follicle

Figure 1-32
Compact Bone   Center of "tree ring" structure, Haversian canal, contains blood vessel. Osteocytes imprisoned in small, dark lacunae surrounding central Haversian canal receive nutrition and communicate via canaliculi, or little canals. Human. (×50)

Haversian canal

Lacunae

Canaliculus

Figure 1-33
Detail of Compact Bone   Haversian system evident.

Canaliculus

Haversian canal

Osteocyte in lacuna

Lamella

Figure 1-34
Cancellous (Spongy) Bone   Osteoblasts on spongy bone are engaged in secretion of new bony matrix. (×100)

Osteoblast

Osteocyte

Resting osteoblast

Spongy bone

Figure 1-35
Red Bone Marrow   Medullary cavity in the head of long bones of the adult contains stem cells and precursors to red and white cells and platelets. Human. (×250)

Cartilage

Figure 1-36
Developing Bone at Epiphyseal Plate
Middle belt of cartilage undergoing primary calcification is replaced by new bone. Secondary ossification occurs later.

Figure 1-37
Detail of Epiphyseal Plate   Epiphyseal plate cartilage at right transforms into zones of proliferating chondrocytes with primary ossification occurring on their calcified remnants. Newly formed bone appears at left. (×50)

Figure 1-38
Striated (Skeletal) Muscle (Cross Section)
Eccentrically located multiple nuclei
accompany individual cells (fibers), each
of which contains many myofibrils.
Human tongue. (×250)

Muscle fibers

Nucleus

Figure 1-39
**Striated (Skeletal) Muscle Fiber
(Longitudinal Section)**   Banded appearance
arises from regular arrangement of
overlapping bundles of thick and thin
filaments (myosin and actin, respectively).
Eccentrically located nuclei are thin
and elongated. (×250)

Nucleus

Figure 1-40
**Striated (Skeletal) Muscle Fibers
(Longitudinal Section)**   Each light (*I*) band
has a dark (*Z*) line through it. Each dark
(*A*) band has a light (*H*) zone through it.
(×250)

H zone

Z line

A band

Nucleus

I band

Figure 1-41
Cardiac Muscle (Longitudinal Section)
Multinucleated, striated muscle fibers branch and anastomose at junctions marked by dark intercalated disks. (×250)

Nucleus

Intercalated disk

Figure 1-42
Smooth Muscle (Longitudinal Section)
Canoe- or spindle-shaped muscle cells lack striations, and each has a single, elongated nucleus. (×250.

Nucleus

Figure 1-43
Innervation of Skeletal Muscle: Motor Endplate   Branching nerve bundle terminates in small, specialized dents, the **myoneural junctions**. Nerve terminals release small quantities of chemical neurotransmitter to stimulate muscle contraction.

Myoneural junction

Figure 1-44
Astrocytes (Neuroglia)   Star-shaped supporting cells of central nervous system modulate ionic environment. Cytoplasmic extensions make contact with blood vessel. Cat. (Silver stain; ×280)

Astrocyte

Blood vessel

Figure 1-45
Purkinje Cells (Neurons)   Numerous branched processes (dendrites) receive information for processing. Single process (axon) sends information to other neurons. Human cerebellum. (×100)

Dendrites

Nucleus

Axon

Figure 1-46
Pyramidal Cells   Neurons from human cortex directly receive information from hundreds of other cells; send information on to hundreds of others. (Fox-Golgi stain; ×100)

Dendrites

Axon

Figure 1-47
Dorsal Root Ganglion   Sensory signals representing pain, temperature, pressure, muscle tension, joint position, and others depend on these cells. Their dendrites and axons collect sensory information throughout the body and route it into the spinal cord. (×100)

Node of Ranvier

Figure 1-48
Nerve Fibers (Longitudinal Section)   Clear areas show dimpling characteristic of nodes of Ranvier. (×250)

Figure 1-49
Motor Neurons of the Spinal Cord
Integrated command information from the brain and sensory signals enter these cells, whose efferent activity controls muscular contraction. Numerous synapses occur on dendrites and soma. (×50)

Figure 1-50
Myelinated Nerve Fibers (Cross Section)
Central core stains dark; insulating myelin
appears white. (×250)

Figure 1-51
Spinal Cord, Lumbar Region (Cross Section)
Top is dorsal, bottom is ventral. Light
central dot is central canal. Darkly staining
H-shaped region is grey matter of cell bodies;
surrounding lighter material is composed of
myelinated axons. Ventral horns of grey
matter contain motor neurons; dorsal horns
contain cell bodies of sensory pathways.
(×4)

White matter
Dorsal horn
Central canal
Ventral horn

Figure 1-52
Retina   Layered structure evident. Dark
line of cells near top is pigment epithelium.
Broad striped region represents
photoreceptors (rods and cones), whose
nuclei stain heavily immediately beneath.
Below receptor nuclei lie synaptic region
and a layer of nuclei belonging to bipolar
cells. Bipolar cell output synapses onto
ganglion cells, only a few of which appear
near bottom. Axons of ganglion cells form
optic nerve. (×100)

Pigmented epithelium
Rods and cones
Receptor nuclei
Bipolar cell nuclei
Ganglion cells

Figure 1-53

Organ of Corti   Thick finger of tectorial membrane extends from right to stimulate complex of four hair cells (three on left, one on right) of central structure that rests on important basilar membrane. Nerve fibers from hair cells exit right to spiral ganglion for processing and transmission of messages to brain. (×100)

Tectorial membrane

Nerve fibers

Hair cells

Basilar membrane

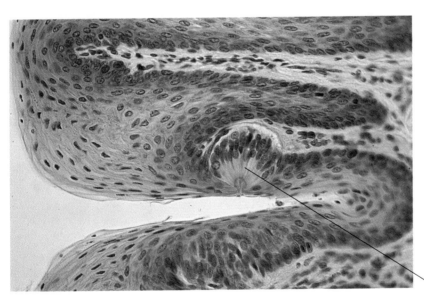

Figure 1-54

Taste Bud   Dissolved chemicals enter fungiform papilla through small pore to directly stimulate sensory cells and initiate taste perception. (×100)

Taste bud

Figure 1-55
Thyroid Gland Follicles   Cuboidal
epithelium surrounds endocrine follicles of
the thyroid gland, the only gland that stores
substantial amounts of its own hormone.
(×100)

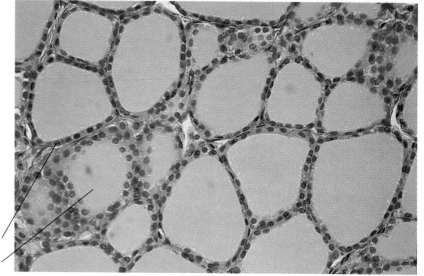

Cuboidal cells

Thyroid follicle

Figure 1-56
Pancreas   The pancreatic islet cells form
the endocrine portion of the pancreas.
Alpha cells secrete glucagon, beta cells
secrete insulin, and delta cells secrete
somatostatin. The exocrine portion of
the pancreas secretes digestive enzymes
through a series of ducts.

Pancreatic islet

Exocrine portion of pancreas

Figure 1-57
Adrenal Cortex   Outer zone of rounded
groups of cells (zona glomerulosa) secretes
mineralcorticosteroids (aldosterone).
Middle area of cell stripes (zona fasciculata)
secretes glucocorticosteroids. Innermost
zone of cells arranged in a meshwork (zona
reticularis) secretes mainly androgens.
(×50)

Zona glomerulosa

Zona fasciculata

Zona reticularis

Figure 1-58
Neutrophil   Most numerous (65%) of the leukocytes, it is characterized by a multilobed nucleus and granular cytoplasm. Engages in phagocytosis. (Neutral dyes stain; ×640)

Nucleus
Barr body

Figure 1-59
Basophil   Normally the rarest (1%) of the leukocytes, its kidney-shaped nucleus may be almost obscured by cytoplasmic granules. These cells contain numerous chemicals involved in inflammation. (Basic dyes stain; ×640)

Figure 1-60
Eosinophil   Relatively rare (6%) leukocyte. Usually identifiable because of red-to-orange-staining cytoplasmic granules. Function not definitely known but elevated especially in allergies. (Selective eosin stain; ×640)

Figure 1-61

Lymphocyte   Common (25%). Characterized by single-lobed, "dented" nucleus surrounded by clear cytoplasm. May be large or small. Heavily involved in the immune response including, for those resident in lymph nodes, synthesis of antibodies. (×640)

Figure 1-62

Monocyte   Relatively rare (3%). Lobed, often kidney-shaped nucleus is surrounded by clear cytoplasm. Largest of the leukocytes, this cell is a scavenger and engages in phagocytosis. (×640)

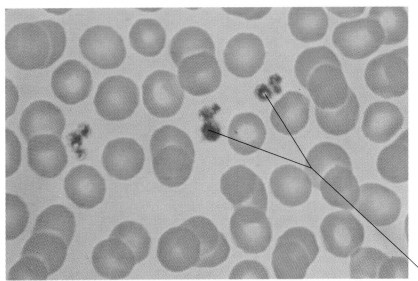

Figure 1-63
Erythrocytes (Red Blood Cells) and Platelets
Circulating erythrocytes are far more common than any of the leukocytes. Normally they have no nucleus but do contain the red pigment hemoglobin, which permits them to transport oxygen and carbon dioxide throughout the body. Typically they assume the shape of a biconcave disk. Their diameter of about 7 microns is useful for comparing sizes of other histological structures. Platelets are cellular remnants of a leukocyte precursor. These remnants contain numerous chemicals, including those important for clotting and inflammation. Platelets initiate blood clotting by forming a plug at wound sites. (×500)

Platelets

Figure 1-64
Sickle Cell Anemia   Genetic alteration of hemoglobin results in altered membrane structure and abnormal wavy or elongated, curved shape that often resembles a sickle (*upper left*). Oxygen-carrying capacity is much reduced. (×500)

Figure 1-65
Artery (A) and Vein (V) Blood vessels possess a **tunica intima** that lines the lumen, outside of which is a muscular **tunica media**, and a connective tissue covering, the **tunica adventitia**. The tunica media of arteries is typically much thicker than that of veins. (×100)

Tunica adventitia
Tunica media
Tunica intima
A
V

Figure 1-66
Arterial Cross Section Single layer of darkly stained cells, the tunica intima, lines the lumen. Thick tunica media is composed of canoe-shaped smooth muscle cells. Outer adventitial layer of connective tissue provides elastic support and strength. (×50)

Tunica media
Tunica adventitia
Lumen
Tunica intima

Figure 1-67

Detail of Arterial Wall   Inner endothelial cells of tunica intima *(left)* lie on a basement membrane. A thin layer of smooth muscle cells and elastic tissue (lamina propria) throws this tunic into folds. The tunica media contains multiple layers of smooth muscle cells regularly arranged. A wavy external elastic membrane separates the tunica media from the adventitia.

Adventitia

Tunica media

Lamina propria

Endothelium and basement membrane

External elastic membrane

Figure 1-68

Capillary with Red Blood Cells in Single File
Capillary wall is made of flattened endothelial cells without complex tunics, a simple structure that facilitates the exchange of gases, nutrients, wastes, and hormones. (×400)

Endothelium

Red blood cell

Figure 1-69

Lymph Node   Outer cortex containing several follicles surrounds medulla, with its narrow, dark medullary cords. Notch is hilum, through which blood and lymphatic vessels pass. (×5)

Follicle (germinal center)

Hilum

Medulla

Cortex

Figure 1-70

Valve of Lymphatic Vessel   One-way flow of lymph, from left to right in this figure, is ensured by valve action in lymph vessel. Vessels themselves are thin walled and lack musculature; pumping action occurs through compression by neighboring muscles. (×25)

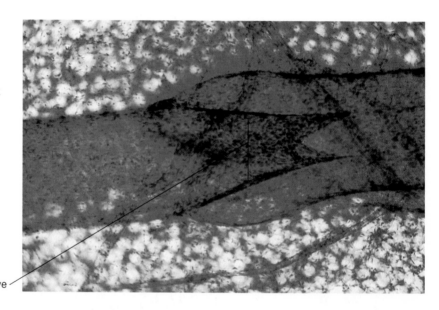

Valve

Figure 1-71

Thymus   Various lobules contain thick, darkly staining cortex surrounding a smaller, lighter-staining medulla. Small, round cellular patches in medulla are Hassall's corpuscles. In adults, much of thymus degenerates and is replaced by adipose tissue. (×10)

Hassall's corpuscle

Figure 1-72
Palatine Tonsil   Outer capsule surrounds subcapsular sinus, under which are several large, rounded germinal centers (lymph nodes) surrounding trabecular arteries and veins. Efferent lymph vessel leads out to upper left. (×5)

Lymph vessel

Germinal center

Figure 1-73
Spleen   Central blood vessels are surrounded by area of densely staining white pulp composed of lymphoid cells. Less densely staining red pulp, with fewer cell nuclei, surrounds white pulp. (×25)

Blood vessels

White pulp

Red pulp

Figure 1-74
Alveoli   Thin-walled respiratory exchange
surfaces aid in rapid diffusion of gases.
Bronchiole terminates at atrium, which
acts as entryway into several individual
alveolar sacs, greatly multiplying surface
area. (×50)

Alveolar sacs

Atrium

Figure 1-75
Detail of Alveolus   Squamous cells
compose alveolar sac, which is penetrated
by thin-walled blood vessels *(upper left)*
containing erythrocytes. (×100)

Blood vessels

Free alveolar macrophage

Erythrocyte

Simple squamous epithelium

Figure 1-76
Bronchiole   Epithelial layer that lines the
lumen is surrounded by layer of smooth
muscle, which regulates bronchiolar
diameter. Round structures outside of
smooth muscle layer are blood vessels.
(×100)

Blood vessel

Smooth muscle

Lumen

Epithelium

Figure 1-77

Esophagus   Surrounding the lumen, esophageal structure contains, in order, the four basic layers of the alimentary canal: **mucosa** (composed of epithelium, the thick lamina propria, and dark muscularis), **submucosa** (light with spaces, blood vessels, and lymph channels), two thick layers of the **muscularis** (circular and longitudinal), and the thin, connective **adventitia** on the surface. Cross section, human. (×3)

Mucosa

Submucosa

Adventitia

Muscularis

Figure 1-78

Stomach Mucosa   Visible at entrances to gastric pits are mucus-secreting goblet cells of columnar epithelium. Deeper in pits are acid-secreting parietal cells and enzyme-secreting chief cells. Endocrine-secreting cells near tip of pits are noncolumnar and smaller, with dark, round nuclei. Gastric pits penetrate deep into submucosal layer. Edge of muscularis layer is visible. (×50)

Endocrine cells

Goblet cells

Parietal cells

Chief cells

Figure 1-79

Small Intestine, Villi of Ileum (Longitudinal Section)   Numerous pale goblet cells punctuate columnar epithelium that composes each villus. Core of villus contains small blood vessels and blind lymph channel (lacteal). Deep in crypts are endocrine cells, identifiable as dark, round nuclei in a noncolumnar cytoplasm. Human. (×50)

Endocrine cells

Blood vessel and lacteal

Goblet cell

Figure 1-80
Small Intestine, Villi of Ileum (Cross Section)
Goblet cells emptying contents through brush border surface are evident. Core of villus contains blood vessels, lymph channels, and lymphocytes. Human. (×100)

Brush border

Goblet cell

Lymphocyte

Figure 1-81
Large Intestine (Colon) (Cross Section)
Surface is thrown into folds but devoid of villi. Thick submucosa contains blood vessels and lymph channels. (×10)

Submucosa

Blood vessel

Lymph channel

Figure 1-82
Liver with Central Vein and Sinusoids
Parenchymal hepatocytes lie in radial arrangement around central vein that is lined with single endothelial layer. Cords of hepatocytes are separated by spaces (sinusoids). Sinusoidal surface is covered by microvilli. (×100)

Sinusoid

Hepatocyte

Central vein

Figure 1-83
Gallbladder   Mucosal folds are covered by epithelium with well-developed microvilli. Lamina propria contains blood vessels. (×25)

Blood vessel

Lamina propria

Muscularis

Figure 1-84
Vermiform Appendix (Cross Section)
Overall structure resembles that of colon.
Large, darkly staining structures are
lymphoid follicles, the size and number of
which decrease with age. Human. (×3)

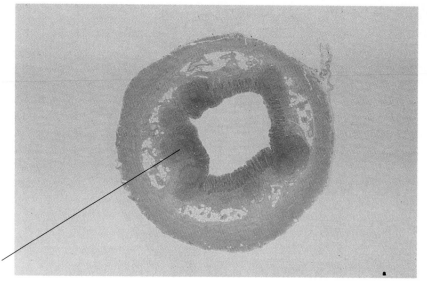

Lymphoid follicle
(germinal center)

Figure 1-85
Sublingual Salivary Gland   Large, pale,
mucus-secreting cells, some with caps of
serous demilunes, secrete their contents
into ducts that may be lined with striated
epithelial cells indicative of ion exchange
activity. (×100)

Epithelial cells
Salivary ducts
Serous demilunes

Figure 1-86
Parotid Salivary Gland   Granular serous cells with numerous, large, zymogen granules surround duct. Several tiny ducts run between clusters within the plane of section. Human. (×100)

Zymogen granule

Salivary duct

Figure 1-87
Submandibular Salivary Gland with Mucous (Light Staining) and Serous (Dark Staining) Components   Striated duct is visible at lower left. (×100)

Duct

Figure 1-88
Bowman's Capsule and Glomerulus (Renal Corpuscle)   Tuft of capillaries, surrounded by podocytes, protrudes into space of Bowman's capsule. Parietal surface is lined with single layer of simple squamous cells. (×100)

Space in Bowman's capsule

Glomerulus

Squamous cell

Figure 1-89
Two Glomeruli and Bowman's Capsules
"Lacy" edges of glomerulus on left shows characteristics of pregnancy-induced hypertension (PIH), here induced experimentally in a pregnant rat. (×50)

Figure 1-90
Distal Convoluted Tubules Lined with Cuboidal Epithelium   Cross section of rat. (×400)

Cuboidal cell

Figure 1-91
Ureter Star-shaped lumen is lined with transitional epithelium that varies in thickness to change shape as lumen stretches. Delicate lamina propria separates epithelium from alternating layers of circular and longitudinal smooth muscle. (×25)

Smooth muscle and adventitial connective tissue

Transitional epithelium

Lamina propria

Figure 1-92
Urinary Bladder Umbrella cells of transitional epithelium stretch and flatten as bladder fills. Basement membrane separates epithelium from underlying connective tissue containing blood vessels. Monkey. (×100)

Umbrella cells

Free surface of bladder

Basement membrane

Blood vessel

Figure 1-93
Urethra (within Penis) Lumen is lined with transitional epithelium and is embedded in corpus spongiosum of the penis. Paraurethral glands located above the lumen in the figure secrete mucus into the urethra. A smooth muscle layer (tunica muscularis) surrounds the urethral structures. (×10)

Paraurethral glands

Corpus spongiosum

Tunica muscularis

Lumen

Figure 1-94
Seminiferous Tubules of Testis Lined with Sertoli Cells and Germinativum in Various Stages of Development   Tunica propria surrounds each tubule. Interstitial spaces contain blood vessels and clumps of interstitial (Leidig) cells that secrete testosterone. ($\times$50)

Sertoli cells

Interstitial cells

Tunica propria

Figure 1-95
Spermatozoa   Head contains numerous enzymes and nucleus with DNA. Thick midpiece just behind head is packed with mitochondria. ($\times$250)

Figure 1-96
Epididymis   Tall, pseudostratified columnar epithelium with microvilli surrounds a lumen packed with clumps of spermatozoa. Narrow band of smooth muscle cells encircles each tubule.

Pseudostratified columnar epithelium

Smooth muscle

Figure 1-97
Ductus Deferens   Ciliated columnar epithelial cells line a spermatozoa-filled lumen. Three layers of smooth muscle cells surround mucosa, a circular layer between two longitudinal ones. (×50)

Columnar epithelium of mucosa

Smooth muscle

Figure 1-98
Prostate Gland   Mucosal surfaces, lined with tall columnar cells and darkly stained basal nuclei, are arranged in numerous deep folds. Lumina open directly into prostatic urethra. Smooth muscle and fibrocollagenous stroma surround luminal structures. Human. (×50)

Columnar epithelium

Smooth muscle and fibrocollagenous bundles

Figure 1-99
Penis   Two corpora cavernosa lie superior to single corpus spongiosum containing penile urethra. Septum between corpora cavernosa is incomplete. Dense fibrous connective tissue, tunica albuginea, surrounds the three vascular cavernosa. The inferior aspect appears on the left, the superior aspect on the right. (×5)

Tunica albuginea

Corpora cavernosa

Corpus spongiosum

Figure 1-100

Ovary with Numerous Primordial Follicles and Two Primary Follicles Primordial follicles contain oocytes that are not stimulated to complete the first meiotic division. Two primary follicles each contain ovum with nucleus and clear surrounding cytoplasm. Thin, clear **zona pellucida** is surrounded by a ring of even cuboidal cells, the **corona radiata**. (×25)

Primary follicles

Primordial follicles

Cytoplasm

Membrane of ovum

Figure 1-101

Detail of Oocyte in Primordial Follicle Clear nucleus contains well-defined nucleolus. Neither zona pellucida nor corona radiata is evident. (×250)

Nucleolus

Nucleus

Figure 1-102

Secondary Ovarian Follicle with Ovum Bright zona pellucida surrounds outer membrane of ovum and in turn is surrounded by dark, cellular corona radiata. A large **antrum** has formed where the egg is not anchored to the follicular wall of **granulosa cells**. (×100)

Nucleus

Membrane of ovum

Zona pellucida

Corona radiata

Antrum

Figure 1-103

Fallopian (Uterine) Tube Extensive folding of mucosa, lined with ciliated columnar epithelium, is common. Epithelium rests on thin basement membrane and flat connective tissue layer. Rhythmic beating of cilia helps transport ovum toward uterus; cell structure also suggests secretory function. Human. (×100)

Columnar epithelium

Connective tissue

Figure 1-104

Uterus Endometrial lining (*right*) during proliferative phase of uterine cycle shows thickening of epithelial surfaces and numerous coiled glandular ducts. (×25)

Endothelial lining

Glandular ducts

Human Skeletal Anatomy

Detail of Compact Bone

Figure 2-1
Skull: Face

BONE

1. Frontal
2. Inferior concha
3. Lacrimal
4. Nasal
5. Parietal
6. Sphenoid
7. Temporal
8. Vomer
9. Zygomatic (malar)
19. Maxilla

FORAMINA

10. Orbital fissure
11. Optic
12. Supraorbital
13. Infraorbital
14. Lacrimal
15. Mental

PROCESSES

16. Mandibular alveolus
17. Maxillary alveolus
18. Perpendicular plate of
    ethmoid
20. Temporal process of malar
21. Zygomatic process of
    maxilla
22. Mandibular ramus
23. Frontal notch
24. Anterior nasal spine

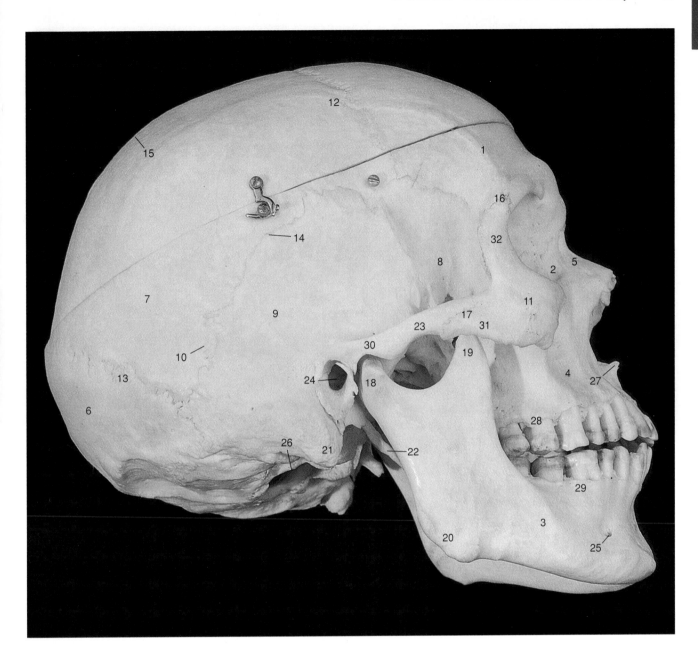

Figure 2-2
Skull: View from Right Side

BONE

1. Frontal
2. Lacrimal
3. Mandible
4. Maxilla
5. Nasal
6. Occipital
7. Parietal
8. Sphenoid (greater wing)
9. Temporal
10. Wormian
11. Zygomatic (malar)

SUTURES

12. Coronal
13. Lambdoidal
14. Squamosal
15. Sagittal
16. Frontozygomatic
17. Temporozygomatic

FORAMINA & PROCESSES

18. Mandibular condyloid process
19. Mandibular coronoid process
21. Mastoid process
22. Styloid process

23. Zygomatic arch
24. External auditory meatus
25. Mental foramen
2. Lacrimal foramen
20. Mandibular angle
26. Foramen magnum
27. Anterior nasal spine
28. Maxillary alveolus
29. Mandibular alveolus
30. Zygomatic process of temporal bone
31. Temporal process of malar
32. Frontal process of malar

Figure 2-3
Skull: Calvarium, Superior Aspect

BONE

1. Frontal
2. Parietal
3. Occipital

SUTURES

4. Coronal
5. Occipital
6. Sagittal
7. Bregma
8. Lambda

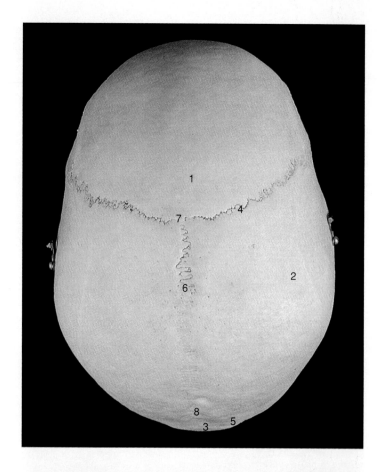

Figure 2-4
Skull: Floor of Cranium, Internal View

BONE

1. Frontal
2. Occipital
3. Parietal
4. Temporal
5. Ethmoid
6. Sphenoid
   (*not shown*)
   Incus
   Malleus
   Stapes

FORAMINA

7. Foramen magnum
8. Foramen ovale
9. Optic foramen
10. Foramen rotundum
11. Foramen lacerum
12. Carotid canal
13. Jugular fossa and
    foramen

14. Internal auditory
    meatus
15. Grooves for transverse
    and sigmoid sinuses
16. Foramen spinosum

PROCESSES

17. Cribriform plate of
    ethmoid
18. Crista galli
19. Lesser wing of
    sphenoid
20. Greater wing of
    sphenoid
21. Sella turcica
22. Petrous portion of
    temporal bone
23. Orbital plate of
    frontal bone
24. Frontal sinus

Figure 2-5
Skull: Base, Viewed from Below

BONE

1. Maxilla (palatine process)
2. Occipital
3. Palatine
4. Temporal
5. Vomer
6. Zygomatic (malar)

FORAMINA

7. Foramen magnum
8. Foramen ovale
22. Foramen lacerum
9. Carotid canal
10. Foramen spinosum
11. Stylomastoid
12. Incisive
13. Palatine
14. Jugular
21. Hypoglossal canal
27. Inferior orbital fissure
29. Zygomatic process of temporal bone
30. Temporal process of malar
31. Condylar fossa and canal

PROCESSES

15. Occipital condyle
16. Mastoid
17. Styloid
18. Medial and lateral pterygoid processes
19. Zygomatic arch
20. Superior nuchal line
23. Occipitosphenoid suture
24. External occipital protruberance
25. Occipitotemporal suture
26. Mandibular fossa
28. Posteriornasal spine
32. External occipital crest
33. Inferior nuchal line
34. Highest nuchal line

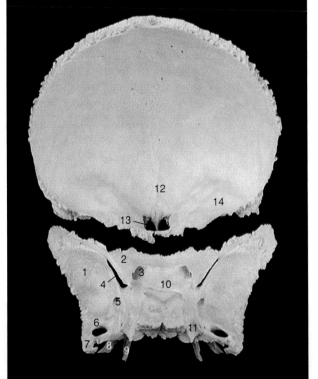

Figure 2-6
Frontal and Sphenoid Bones: Internal Aspect, Frontosphenoidal Suture Separated

PROCESSES

1. Greater wing
2. Lesser wing
8. Lateral pterygoid
9. medial pterygoid
10. Sella turcica
11. Carotid groove
12. Frontal crest
14. Orbital plate

FORAMINA

3. Optic foramen
4. Superior orbital fissure
5. Foramen rotundum
6. Foramen ovale
7. Foramen spinosum
13. Ethmoidal notch

Figure 2-7
Spehnoid: From the Front

PROCESSES

1. Orbital surface
2. Rostrum
7. Medial pterygoid
8. Lateral pterygoid
11. Temporal surface

FORAMINA

3. Optic
4. Superior orbital fissure
5. Foramen rotundum
6. Pterygoid canal
9. Foramen ovale
10. Foramen spinosum

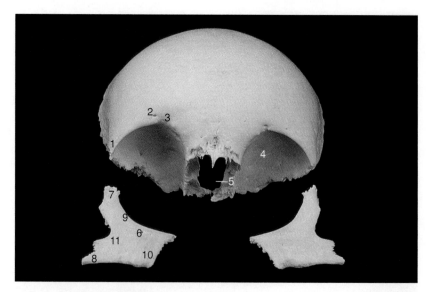

Figure 2-8
Frontal and Zygomatic Bones: From the Front

PROCESSES

1. Zygomatic process
4. Orbit
7. Frontal process
8. Temporal process
9. Orbital border
10. Maxillary border
11. Temporal border

NOTE: Supraorbital foramen and notch on right side are separate; on left they are superimposed.

FORAMINA

2. Supraorbital foramen
3. Supraorbital notch
5. Ethmoidal notch
6. Infraorbital foramen

Figure 2-9
Right Temporal and Parietal Bones: Exterior Aspect, Squamosal Suture Separated

PROCESSES

1. Parietal notch
2. External auditory meatus
3. Zygomatic process
4. Mandibular fossa
5. Mastoid process
6. Styloid process
7. Squamosal border
8. Frontal border
9. Occipital border
10. Suprameatal triangle

Figure 2-10
Left Temporal and Parietal Bones: Interior Aspect, Squamosal Suture Separated

PROCESSES

1. Parietal notch
2. Internal auditory meatus
3. Petrous portion
4. Groove for sigmoid sinus
5. Mastoid process
6. Styloid process
7. Squamosal border
8. Frontal border
9. Occipital border
10. Sagittal border
11. Furrows for frontal branch of middle meningeal vessels
12. Furrows for parietal branch of middle meningeal vessels

Figure 2-11
Occipital Bone: Interior Aspect

PROCESSES

1. Foramen magnum
2. Condylar fossa and canal
3. Jugular notch
4. Groove for sigmoid sinus
5. Jugular tubercle
6. Mastoid margin
7. Internal occipital crest
8. Internal occipital protuberance
9. Groove for transverse sinus
10. Groove for superior sagittal sinus
11. Lambdoidal margin
12. Cerebellar fossa
13. Cerebral fossa

Figure 2-12
Palatine Bones: (A) Right from Anteriomedial View, (B) Left from Anteriosuperior View

PROCESSES

A. Right palatine bone
B. Left palatine bone
1. Orbital process
2. Sphenopalatine notch
3. Sphenoidal process
4. Horizontal plate
5. Ethmoidal crest
6. Pyramidal process
7. Maxillary process
8. Vertical plate

Figure 2-13
Maxillae: (A) Left from Lateral Aspect,
(B) Right from Medial Aspect

PROCESSES

A. Left maxilla
B. Right maxilla
1. Zygomatic process
2. Ethmoidal crest
3. Infraorbital foramen
4. Orbital surface
5. Infratemporal surface
6. Canine fossa
7. Canine eminence
8. Incisive fossa
9. Anterior nasal spine
10. Anterior lacrimal crest
11. Nasolacrimal groove
12. Maxillary hiatus and sinus
13. Palatine process
14. Nasal crest
15. Frontal process
16. Middle meatus
17. Inferior meatus
18. Alveolar process
19. Greater palatine canal

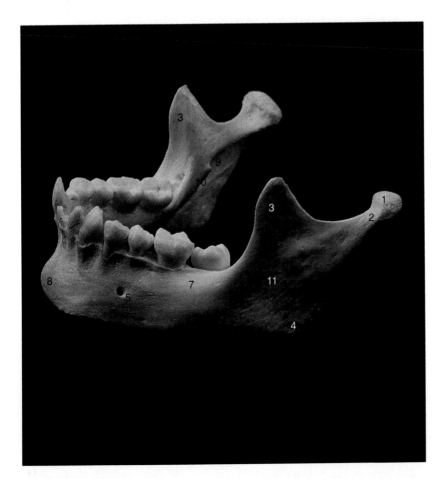

Figure 2-14
Mandible: Left Lateral View

PROCESSES

1. Mandibular condyle
2. Condyloid process
3. Coronoid process
4. Angle
5. Mental foramen
6. Alveolar process
7. Body of mandible
8. Mental protuberance
9. Mandibular foramen
10. Lingula
11. Ramus

Figure 2-15
Ethmoid Bone:
(A) from Above, Right, and Behind
(B) from Below, Right, and Behind

PROCESSES

1. Crista galli
2. Cribriform plate
3. Orbital plate
4. Ethmoidal labyrinth (with air cells)
5. Perpendicular plate
6. Middle nasal concha

Figure 2-16
Spinal Column: View from
Left and Behind

STRUCTURES

A. Atlas
B. Axis
C. 7 Cervical vertebrae
(Arrow near C—Cervical
curvature)
D. Mentum nuchae
(spinous process of 7th cervical
vertebra)
E. 12 Thoracic vertebrae
(Arrow near E—Thoracic
curvature)
F. 5 Lumbar vertebrae
(Arrow near F—Lumbar
curvature)
G. 5 Fused sacral vertebrae
(Arrow near G—Sacral
curvature)
(Not shown 4–5 coccyx)
H. Intervertebral disk
I. Spinous processes
J. Transverse processes
K. Intervertebral foramen

Figure 2-17
Vertebrae

PROCESSES

A. Atlas
B. Axis
C. Cervical vertebra
D. 7th cervical vertebra
E. Thoracic vertebra
F. Lumbar vertebra

1. Body
   (Heavy arrows—Vertebral
   arches—comprised of lamina and
   pedicle)
2. Bifid spinous process
3. Monofid spinous process
4. Lamina

5. Pedicle
6. Odontoid process (dens)
7. Superior articular process and facet
8. Transverse foramen
9. Transverse process
10. Vertebral foramen
11. Costal facet

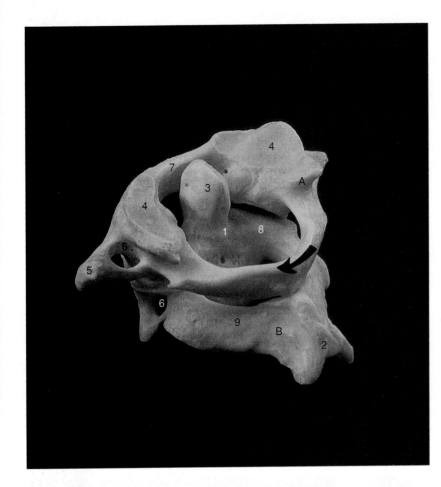

Figure 2-18
(A) Atlas and (B) Axis Articulated

PROCESSES

1. Body of axis
2. Bifid spinous process
3. Odontoid process (dens)
4. Superior articular facet
5. Transverse process
6. Transverse foramen
7. Anterior arch of atlas
   (Heavy arrow—Posterior arch of atlas)
8. Pedicle of axis
9. Lamina of axis

Figure 2-19
Sacrum: (A) Anterior Aspect, (B) Posterior Aspect

PROCESSES

1. Superior articular process and facet
2. Auricular surface
3. Sacral foramen
4. Sacral canal
5. Sacral hiatus
6. Sacral promontory
7. Median crest
8. Lateral crest
9. Site of fusion of 1st and 2nd sacral vertebrae

Figure 2-20
Sternum and Ribs

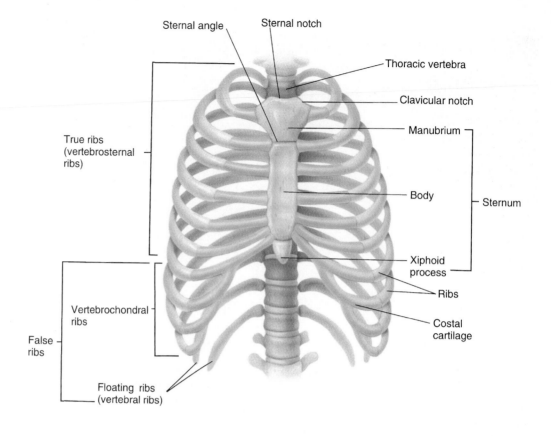

Figure 2-21
Ribs: (A) 1st, (B) 2nd, Right Side, Superior View, (C) 7th, Right Side, Inferior View

PROCESSES

1. Head
2. Neck
3. Articular facet
4. Tubercle
5. Angle
6. Subclavian groove
7. Scalene tubercle
8. Body
9. Costal groove
10. Serratus anterior tuberosity
11. Site for attachment of scalenus medius
12. Site for attachment of levator costa

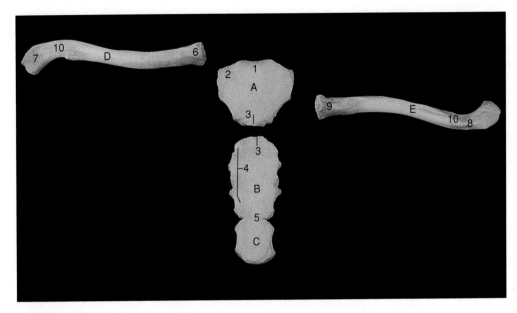

Figure 2-22
Sternum and Clavicles:
Sternum from the Front, (D)
Right Clavicle from Above,
(E) Left Clavicle from
Below

PROCESSES

A. Manubrium
B. Gladiolus (body)
C. Xiphoid process
1. Jugular notch
2. Clavicular notch
3. Sternal angle and
   manubriosternal joint
4. Notches for costal
   cartilages (2–7)
5. Xiphisternal joint
D. Right clavicle
E. Left clavicle
6. Sternal end
7. Acromial end
8. Conoid tubercle
9. Site for costaclavicular
   ligament
10. Site for deltoid

Figure 2-23
Scapulare: (A) Right
Scapula, Anterior View
(B) Left Scapula, Posterior
View

PROCESSES

A. Right scapula
B. Left scapula
1. Coracoid process
2. Acromion
3. Spine
4. Suprascapular notch
5. Superior border
6. Superior angle
7. Medial (vertebral)
   border
8. Lateral (axillary)
   border
9. Infraspinous fossa
10. Supraspinous fossa
11. Subscapular fossa
12. Glenoid fossa
13. Acromial angle
14. Inferior angle

Figure 2-24
Humerus with Scapulae:
(A) Right Humerus, Anterior View
(B) Left Humerus, Posterior View

PROCESSES

A. Right humerus and scapula
B. Left humerus and scapula
 1. Proximal head (epiphysis)
 2. Anatomical neck
 3. Surgical neck
 4. Shaft (diaphysis)
 5. Lesser tubercle
 6. Greater tubercle
 7. Intertubercular groove
 8. Deltoid tuberosity
 9. Acromion
10. Coracoid process
11. Lateral epicondyle
12. Capitulum
13. Trochlea
14. Medial epicondyle
15. Coronoid fossa
16. Olecranon fossa
17. Distal head and surgical neck

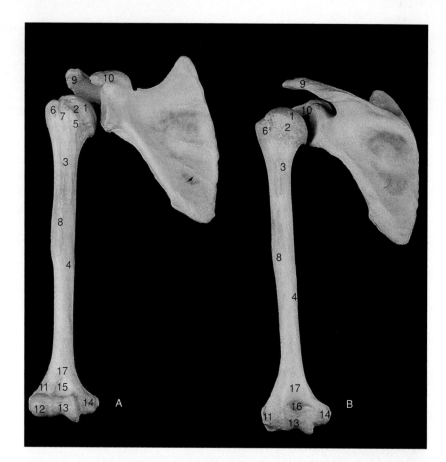

Figure 2-25
Ulna and Radius: Right, Anterior View
Left, Posterior View

PROCESSES

A. Right radius
B. Right ulna
C. Left radius
D. Left ulna
 1. Proximal head
 2. Neck
 3. Radial tuberosity
 4. Anterior oblique line
 5. Interosseous border
 6. Styloid process of radius
 7. Ulnar notch
 8. Olecranon process
 9. Trochlear notch
10. Coronoid process
11. Ulnar tuberosity
12. Styloid process of ulna
13. Distal head
14. Distal neck
15. Radial notch

Figure 2-26
Left Hand, Dorsal View

BONES AND PROCESSES

CARPALS
1. Navicular (scaphoid)
2. Lunate
3. Triangular (triquetrum)
4. Pisiform
5. Greater multangular (trapezium)
6. Lesser multangular (trapezoid)
7. Capitate
8. Hamate
9. METACARPALS 1–5

PHALANGES
10. Proximal phalanx of thumb
11. Distal phalanx of thumb
12. Proximal phalanx of digits 2–5
13. Middle phalanx of digits 2–5
14. Distal phalanx of digits 2–5

Figure 2-27
Pelvic Bones with Sacrum, Anterior View

PROCESSES
1. Iliac crest
2. Anterior superior iliac spine
3. Anterior inferior iliac spine
4. Acetabulum
5. Acetabular notch
6. Obturator foramen
7. Posterior superior iliac spine
8. Posterior inferior iliac spine
9. Ischial spine
10. Iliac fossa
11. Ischial tuberosity
12. Superior pubic ramus
13. Inferior pubic ramus
14. Pubic tubercle
15. Symphysis pubis
16. Pubic arch
17. Iliopectineal line
18. Ischial ramus
19. Iliopubic eminence
20. Fusion of ischium and pubis

Figure 2-28
Pelvic Bones:
(A) Right Innominate, Lateral View
(B) Left Innominate, Medial View

PROCESSES

1. Iliac crest
2. Anterior superior iliac spine
3. Anterior inferior iliac spine
4. Acetabulum
5. Acetabular notch
6. Obturator foramen
7. Posterior superior iliac spine
8. Posterior inferior iliac spine
9. Ischial spine
10. Iliac fossa
11. Ischial tuberosity
12. Superior pubic ramus
13. Inferior pubic ramus
14. Auricular surface (for sacroiliac joint)
15. Symphysis pubis
16. Greater sciatic notch
17. Iliopectineal line
18. Ischial ramus
19. Iliopubic eminence
20. Fusion of ischium and pubis
21. Lesser sciatic notch

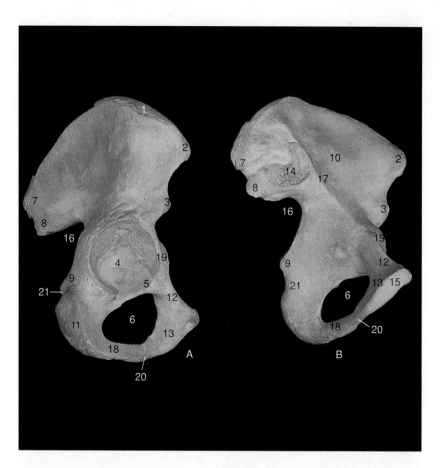

Figure 2-29
Femur: (A) Right Femur, Anterior View
(B) Left Femur, Posterior View

PROCESSES

A. Right femur
B. Left femur
1. Proximal head (epiphysis)
2. Anatomical neck
3. Surgical neck
4. Greater trochanter
5. Lesser trochanter
6. Intertrochanteric crest
7. Spiral line
8. Gluteal tuberosity
9. Linea aspera
10. Lateral condyle
11. Medial condyle
12. Popliteal surface
13. Intercondylar fossa
14. Patellar surface
15. Shaft (diaphysis)
16. Distal head and neck
17. Medial epicondyle
18. Lateral epicondyle
19. Site for attachment of anterior cruciate ligament
20. Site for attachment of posterior cruciate ligament

Figure 2-30
Patellae: (A) Right Patella, Anterior Surface
(B) Left Patella, Posterior (Articular) Surface

PROCESSES

A. Right patella
B. Left patella
 1. Base
 2. Apex (site for attachment of patellar ligament)
 3. Facet for lateral condyle of femur
 4. Vertical ridge
 5. Facet for medial condyle of femur

Figure 2-31
Tibia and Fibula: (A,B) Right Tibia and Fibula, Anterior View
(C,D) Left Tibia and Fibula, Posterior View

PROCESSES

A. Right fibula
B. Right tibia
C. Left fibula
D. Left tibia
 1. Tubercles of intercondylar eminence
 2. Tibial tuberosity
 3. Medial condyle
 4. Lateral condyle
 5. Interosseous border
 6. Soleal line
 7. Articular facet for fibula
 8. Site for posterior cruciate ligament
 9. Medial malleolus
 10. Groove for tibialis posterior
 11. Groove for flexor hallicus longus
 12. Lateral malleolus
 13. Groove for peroneus brevis
 14. Malleolar fossa
 15. Articular facet for tibia
 16. Apex (styloid process)

Figure 2-32
Right Foot: Dorsal (Superior) View

BONES AND PROCESSES

TARSALS
1. Calcaneus
2. Trochlear (articular) surface of talus
3. Lateral tubercle of talus
4. Medial tubercle of talus
5. Groove for flexor hallicus longus
6. Neck of talus
7. Head of talus
8. Navicular
9. Navicular tuberosity
10. Medial cuneiform
11. Intermediate cuneiform
12. Lateral cuneiform
13. Cuboid
14. METATARSALS 1–5

PHALANGES
15. Proximal phalanx of great toe
16. Distal phalanx of great toe
17. Proximal phalanx of digits 2–5
18. Middle phalanx of digits 2–5
19. Distal phalanx of digits 2–5
20. Site for attachment of Achilles tendon

Figure 2-33
Typical Long Bone Structure

PROCESSES

1. Proximal head (epiphysis)
2. Anatomical neck (growth plate, metaphysis, epiphyseal plate)
3. Surgical neck
4. Shaft (diaphysis)
5. Compact bone
6. Cancellous (spongy) bone
7. Distal head
8. Medullary (marrow) cavity

Human Muscular Anatomy

Cardiac Muscle (Longitudinal Section)

Frontalis
Orbicularis oculi
Zygomaticus
Masseter
Orbicularis oris
Trapezius
Sternocleidomastoid
Latissimus dorsi
Deltoid
Serratus anterior
Pectoralis major
External oblique
Biceps brachii
Rectus abdominis
Linea alba
Brachioradialis
Tensor fasciae latae
Sartorius
Iliopsoas
Rectus femoris
Pectineus
Adductor longus
Vastus lateralis
Gracilis
Patellar tendon
Vastus medialis
Peroneus longus
Extensor digitorum longus
Gastrocnemius
Tibialis anterior
Soleus

Figure 3-1
Superficial Skeletal Muscles
A. Anterior view.

Temporalis

Occipitalis

Sternocleidomastoid

Trapezius

Deltoid

Teres minor

Teres major

Triceps brachii

Brachioradialis

Biceps femoris

Semitendinosus

Semimembranosus

Gastrocnemius

Calcaneal tendon

Brachialis

Infraspinatus

Rhomboideus

Latissimus dorsi

External oblique

Gluteus medius

Gluteus maximus

Adductor magnus

Gracilis

Vastus lateralis

Sartorius

Soleus

Peroneus longus

Figure 3-1—cont'd.
B. Posterior view.

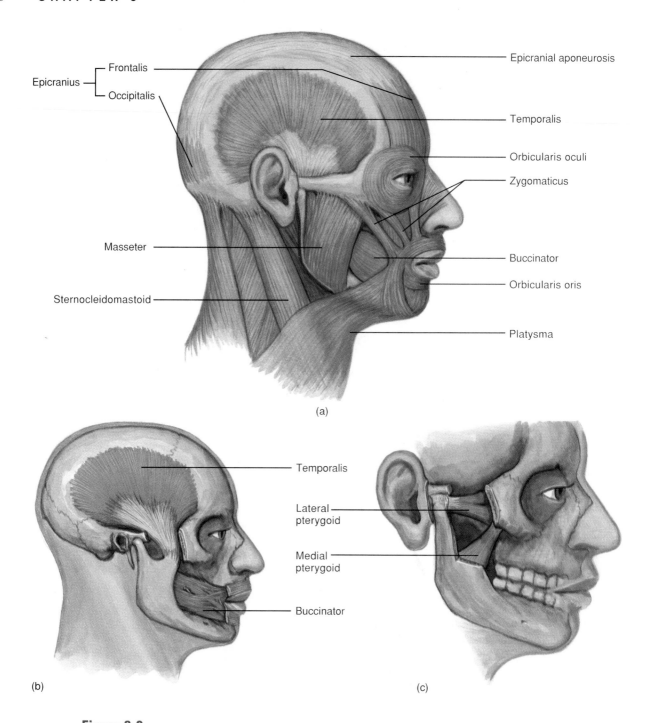

Epicranial aponeurosis

Temporalis

Orbicularis oculi

Zygomaticus

Buccinator

Orbicularis oris

Platysma

Epicranius — Frontalis
Occipitalis

Masseter

Sternocleidomastoid

(a)

Temporalis

Lateral pterygoid

Medial pterygoid

Buccinator

(b)   (c)

Figure 3-2

(a) Muscles of facial expression and mastication; isolated views of (b) the temporalis and buccinator muscles and (c) the lateral medial pterygoid muscles.

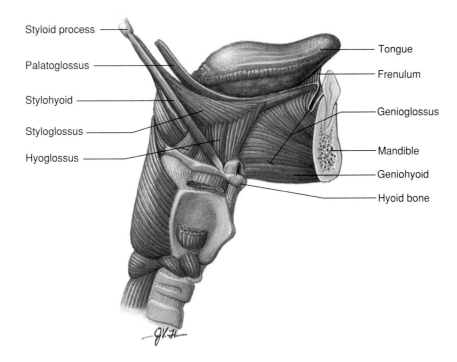

Styloid process
Palatoglossus
Stylohyoid
Styloglossus
Hyoglossus

Tongue
Frenulum
Genioglossus
Mandible
Geniohyoid
Hyoid bone

Figure 3-3
Muscles of the tongue, right lateral view.

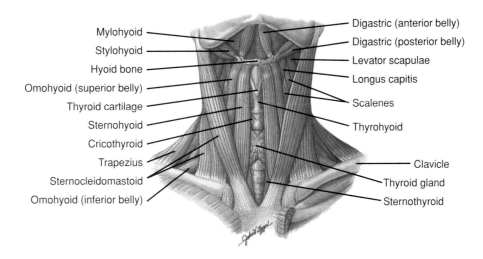

Mylohyoid
Stylohyoid
Hyoid bone
Omohyoid (superior belly)
Thyroid cartilage
Sternohyoid
Cricothyroid
Trapezius
Sternocleidomastoid
Omohyoid (inferior belly)

Digastric (anterior belly)
Digastric (posterior belly)
Levator scapulae
Longus capitis
Scalenes
Thyrohyoid
Clavicle
Thyroid gland
Sternothyroid

Figure 3-4
Muscles of the anterior neck, superficial view.

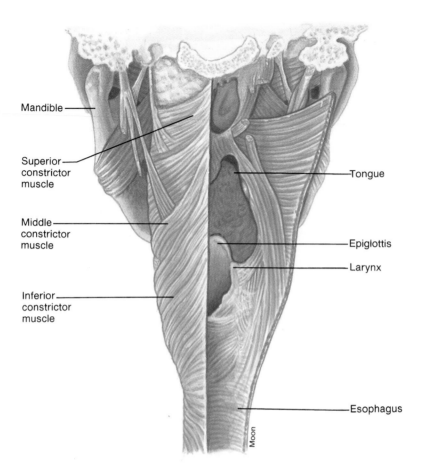

Figure 3-5

Posterior view of the constrictor muscles of the pharynx. Right side has been cut away to illustrate the interior structures in the pharynx.

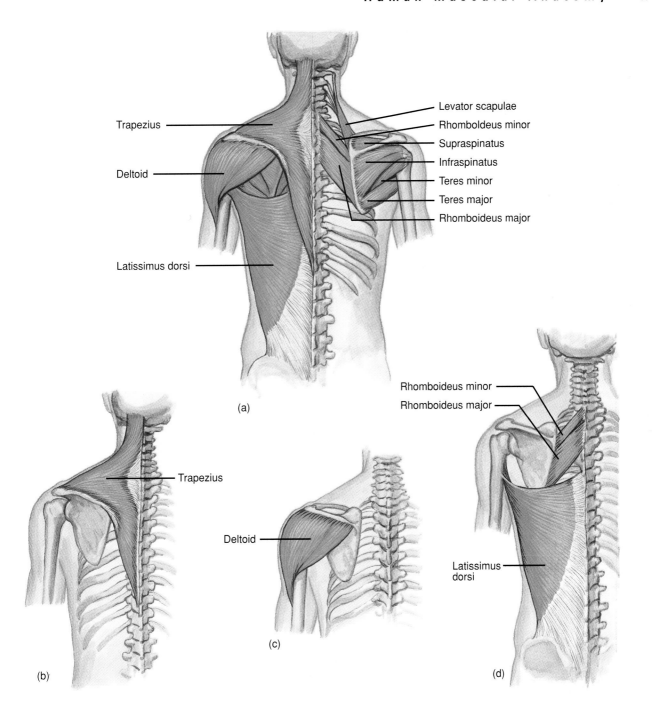

Trapezius

Levator scapulae
Rhomboldeus minor
Supraspinatus
Infraspinatus
Teres minor
Teres major
Rhomboideus major

Deltoid

Latissimus dorsi

(a)

Trapezius

Rhomboideus minor
Rhomboideus major

Deltoid

Latissimus
dorsi

(b)

(c)

(d)

Figure 3-6

(a) Muscles of the posterior shoulder. The right trapezius is
removed to show underlying muscles. Isolated views of (b)
trapezius, (c) deltoid, and (d) rhomboideus and latissimus
dorsi muscles.

Splenius capitis (cut)

Longissimus capitis

Semispinalis capitis (cut)

Longissimus cervicis

Iliocostalis cervicis

Longissimus thoracis

Semispinalis capitis

Spinalis capitis

Splenius capitis

Spinalis cervicis

Iliocostalis thoracis

Spinalis thoracis

Iliocostalis lumborum

Figure 3-7
Deep muscles of the back and the neck help move the head (posterior view) and hold
the torso erect. The splenius capitis and semispinalis capitis are removed on the left to
show underlying muscles.

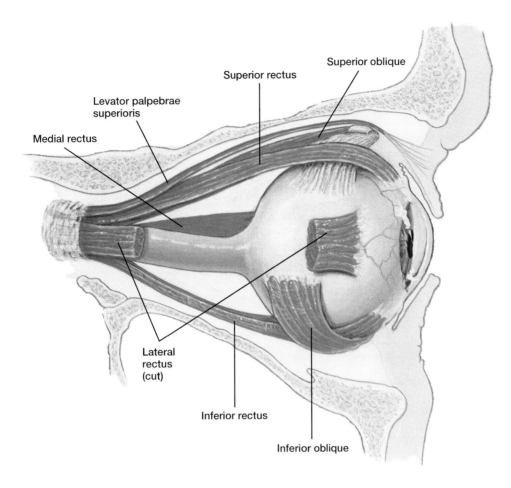

Figure 3-8
Extrinsic muscles of the right eye, lateral view.

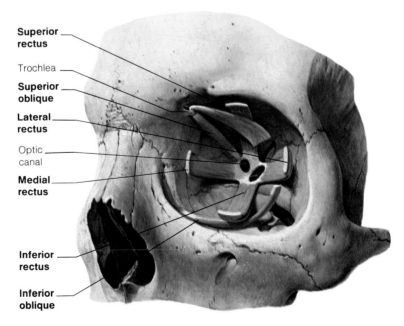

Figure 3-9
Extrinsic muscles of the left eye, anterior view.

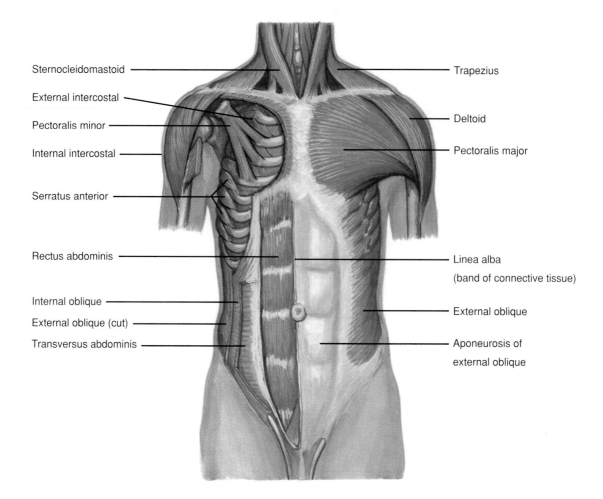

Sternocleidomastoid

External intercostal

Pectoralis minor

Internal intercostal

Serratus anterior

Rectus abdominis

Internal oblique

External oblique (cut)

Transversus abdominis

Trapezius

Deltoid

Pectoralis major

Linea alba
(band of connective tissue)

External oblique

Aponeurosis of
external oblique

Figure 3-10
Muscles of the anterior chest and abdominal wall. The
right pectoralis major is removed to show the pectoralis
minor.

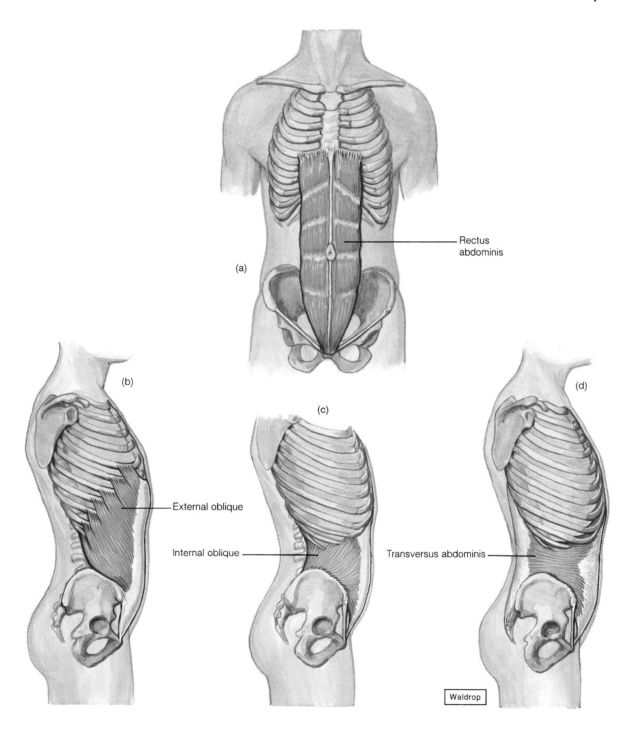

Rectus abdominis

(a)

(b)

(c)

(d)

External oblique

Internal oblique

Transversus abdominis

Waldrop

Figure 3-11
(a–d) Isolated muscles of the abdominal wall.

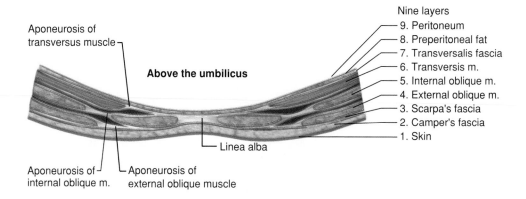

Above the umbilicus

Aponeurosis of
transversus muscle

Nine layers

9. Peritoneum
8. Preperitoneal fat
7. Transversalis fascia
6. Transversis m.
5. Internal oblique m.
4. External oblique m.
3. Scarpa's fascia
2. Camper's fascia
1. Skin

Linea alba

Aponeurosis of
internal oblique m.

Aponeurosis of
external oblique muscle

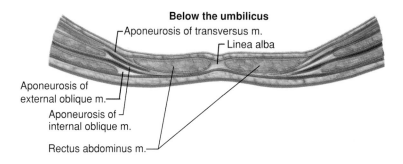

Below the umbilicus

Aponeurosis of transversus m.

Linea alba

Aponeurosis of
external oblique m.

Aponeurosis of
internal oblique m.

Rectus abdominus m.

Figure 3-12

Muscles of the anterior abdominal wall, cross-sectional
view above the umbilicus.

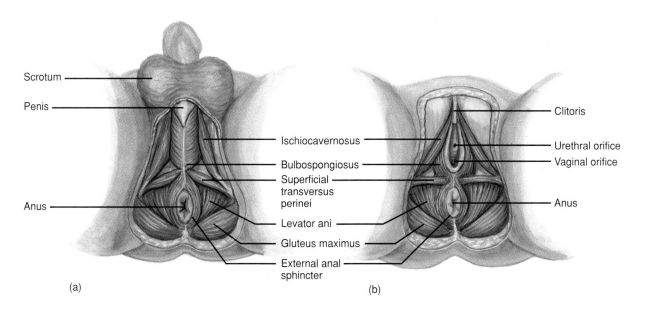

Scrotum

Penis

Anus

Ischiocavernosus

Bulbospongiosus

Superficial transversus perinei

Levator ani

Gluteus maximus

External anal sphincter

(a)

Clitoris

Urethral orifice

Vaginal orifice

Anus

(b)

Coccygeus

Levator ani

Urogenital diaphragm

(c)

Coccyx

Rectum

Vagina

Urethra

Symphysis publis

Figure 3-13

External view of muscles of (a) the male pelvic outlet, and (b) the female pelvic outlet.
(c) Internal view of pelvic and urogenital diaphragms.

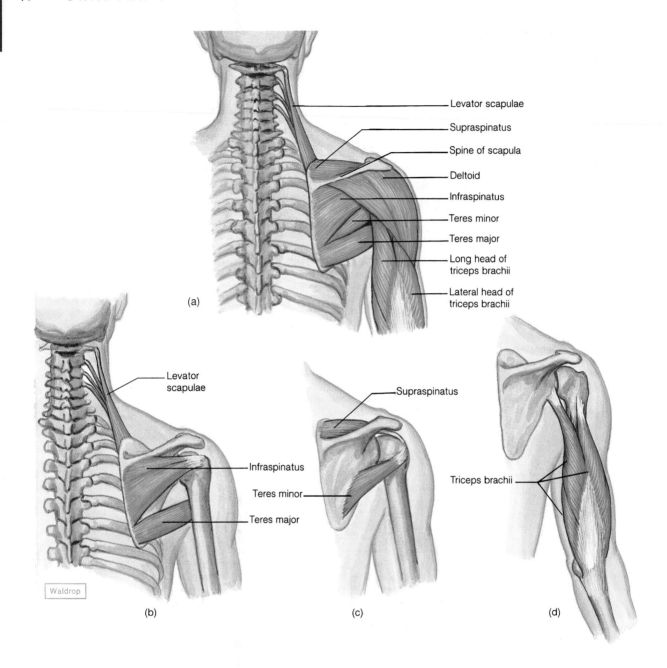

Levator scapulae
Supraspinatus
Spine of scapula
Deltoid
Infraspinatus
Teres minor
Teres major
Long head of triceps brachii
Lateral head of triceps brachii

(a)

Levator scapulae
Infraspinatus
Teres minor
Teres major

(b)

Supraspinatus

(c)

Triceps brachii

(d)

Waldrop

Figure 3-14
(a) Muscles of the posterior surface of the scapula and the arm; (b and c) muscles associated with the scapula. (d) Isolated view of the triceps brachii.

Trapezius
Clavicle
Deltoid
Subscapularis
Coracobrachialis
Short head of biceps brachii
Medial border of scaupla
Long head of biceps brachii
Brachialis

(a)

Biceps brachii (short and long heads)

(b)

Coracobrachialis

Subscapularis

Brachialis

(c)

(d)

Figure 3-15
(a) Muscles of the anterior shoulder and the arm, with the rib cage removed.
(b, c, and d) Isolated views of muscles associated with the arm.

Biceps brachii

Brachialis

Supinator

Pronator teres

Brachioradialis

Extensor carpi radialis longus

Flexor carpi radialis

Palmaris longus

Flexor carpi ulnaris

Pronator quadratus

Flexor digitorum superficialis

Brachioradialis

Flexor carpi ulnaris

Figure 3-16
(a) Muscles of the anterior forearm. (b–e) Isolated views of muscles associated with the anterior forearm.

(a)

(b)

Pronator teres

Pronator quadratus

Flexor digitorum superficialis

Flexor carpi radialis

(c)

(d)

(e)

Triceps brachii

Brachioradialis

Extensor carpi radialis longus

Extensor carpi radialis brevis

Flexor carpi ulnaris

Extensor digitorum

Extensor carpi ulnaris

Extensor retinaculum

(a)

Extensor carpi radialis longus and brevis

(b)

Extensor carpi ulnaris

Extensor digitorum

(c)

Figure 3-17
(a) Muscles of the posterior forearm. (b and c) Isolated views of muscles associated with the posterior forearm.

Psoas major

Iliacus

Tensor fasciae latae

Fascia

Sartorius

Rectus femoris

Vastus lateralis

Patella

Adductor longus

Adductor magnus

Gracilis

Vastus medialis

Patellar ligament

(a)

Sartorius

Vastus intermedius

(b)

Gracilis

(c)

Adductor longus

(d)

Adductor magnus

(e)

Psoas major

(f)

Iliacus

(g)

Figure 3-18

(a) Muscles of the anterior
right thigh. Isolated views of
(b) the vastus intermedius;
(c–e) adductors of the thigh;
(f–g) flexors of the thigh.

Gluteus medius

Gluteus maximus

Biceps femoris
long head
short head

Tensor fasciae latae

Sartorius

Rectus femoris

Vastus lateralis

Fascia at
iliotibial band

(a)

Gluteus
medius

Gluteus
maximus

Gluteus
minimus

(b)   (c)   (d)

Figure 3-19
(a) Muscles of the lateral right thigh. (b–d) Isolated views of the gluteal muscles.

Gluteus medius

Gluteus maximus

Adductor magnus

Vastus lateralis
covered by fascia

Gracilis

Semitendinosus

Biceps femoris

Semimembranosus

Sartorius

Gastrocnemius

(a)

Semimembranosus

Biceps femoris
(short head)

(b)

Semitendinosus

Biceps femoris
(long head)

(c)

Figure 3-20
(a) Muscles of the posterior right thigh. (b and c) Isolated
views of muscles that flex the leg at the knee.

Patella

Patellar ligament

Tibialis anterior

Peroneus longus

Extensor digitorum longus

Peroneus brevis

Gastrocnemius

Soleus

Tibia

Extensor hallicus longus

Extensor retinacula

(a)

Tibialis anterior

Peroneus tertius

Extensor hallicus longus

Extensor digitorum longus

(b)

(c)

(d)

Figure 3-21

(a) Muscles of the anterior right leg. (b–d) Isolated views of muscles associated with the anterior leg.

Biceps femoris
long head
short head

Vastus lateralis

Head of fibula

Gastrocnemius

Tibialis anterior

Soleus

Peroneus longus

Extensor digitorum longus

Calcaneal tendon

Peroneus brevis

Peroneus
tertius

Extensor retinacula

Peroneal
retinacula

(a)

Peroneus longus

Peroneus brevis

(b)

(c)

Figure 3-22

(a) Muscles of the lateral right leg. Isolated views of
(b) peroneus longus and (c) peroneus brevis.

Semitendinosus

Semimembranosus

Gracilis

Sartorius

Biceps femoris

(a)

(b)

Gastrocnemius:

Medial head

Lateral head

Peroneus longus

Gastrocnemius

Soleus

Calcaneal tendon

Peroneus brevis

Flexor digitorum
longus

Flexor
retinaculum

Calcaneus

Peroneal retinacula

(c)

Plantaris

Soleus

(d)

Tibialis posterior

Flexor digitorum
longus

(e)

Figure 3-23

(a) Muscles of the posterior right leg. (b–e) Isolated
views of muscles associated with the posterior right leg.

Anterior tibial artery and deep fibular nerve

Tendon of tibialis anterior

Medial melleolus

Anterior medial malleolar artery

Tendon of extensor hallucis longus

Dorsalis pedis artery

Deep peroneal nerve

Extensor hallucis brevis

Arcuate artery

Abductor hallucis

First dorsal interosseous

Tendon of extensor hallucis brevis

Extensor expansions

Dorsal digital arteries

Dorsal digital branches of superficial peroneal nerve

Superior extensor retinaculum

Peroneus tertius

Tendon of extensor digitorum longus

Lateral malleolus

Inferior extensor retinaculum

Tendon of peroneus brevis

Extensor digitorum brevis

Tendon of peroneus tertius

Tuberosity of fifth metatarsal bone

Abductor digiti minimi

Tendons of extensor digitorum brevis

Tendons of extensor digitorum longus

Figure 3-24
Dorsum of the foot, anterior view.

4

Dissections

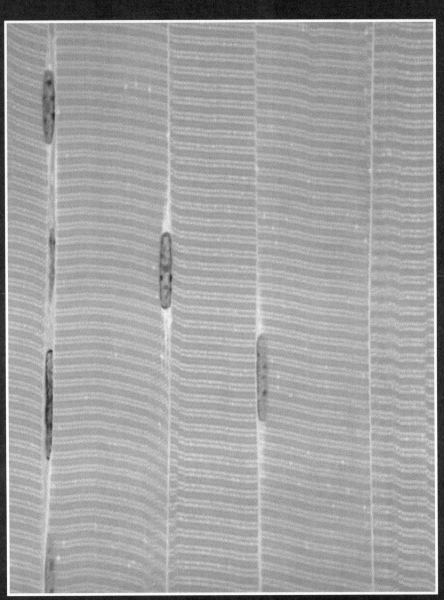

Striated (Skeletal) Muscle Fibers (Longitudinal Section)

Figure 4-1
The Cat Skeleton
1. Maxilla
2. Mandible
3. Orbit
4. Zygomatic arch
5. Cranium
6. Cervical vertebrae (7)
7. Sternum
8. Scapula
9. Humerus
10. Radius
11. Ulna
12. Carpal bones
13. Metacarpal bones
14. Phalanges
15. Thoracic vertebrae (13)
16. Ribs
17. Lumbar vertebrae (7)
18. Pelvis
19. Femur
20. Tibia
21. Fibula
22. Calcaneus
23. Tarsal bones
24. Metatarsal bones
25. Phalanges
26. Caudal vertebrae (21–25)

Figure 4-2
Cat Skull, Left Lateral View

A. Mandible
   1. Lower canine tooth
   2. Mental foramina
   3. Lower premolar teeth
   4. Lower molar teeth
   5. Angular process
   6. Condyloid process
   7. Coronoid process
B. Incisive bone
C. Nasal bone
D. Maxilla
   8. Upper canine tooth
   9. Infraorbital foramen
   10. Upper premolar tooth
   11. Upper molar tooth

E. Lacrimal bone and fossa
F. Orbit
G. Frontal bone
   12. Zygomatic process of frontal bone
H. Coronal suture
I. Malar or zygomatic bone
   13. Frontal process of malar
   14. Temporal process of malar
J. Temporal bone
   15. Zygomatic process of temporal bone
   16. External auditory meatus
   17. Stylomastoid foramen
   18. Mastoid process

K. Parietal bone
L. Squamosal suture
M. Occipital bone
   19. External occipital protuberance
   20. Nuchal crest
   21. Occipital condyle
N. Atlas
O. Axis
P. Cervical vertebrae (3–7)
   22. Spinous process
   23. Transverse process
   24. Transverse foramen

Figure 4-3
Axial Skeleton of Cat, Dorsal View

1. Frontal bone
2. Parietal bone
3. Sagittal suture
4. Coronal suture
5. Bregma
6. Atlas
7. Transverse process (wing) of atlas
8. Axis
9. Cervical vertebrae (7)
10. Thoracic vertebrae (13)
11. Ribs
12. Lumbar vertebrae (7)
13. Sacral vertebrae (3)
14. Caudal vertebrae (21–25)
15. Scapula
16. Humerus
17. Ilium
18. Ischium
19. Femur

Figure 4-4
Cat Skeleton, Front Right Lateral Aspect

A. Vertebral spinous process
B. Sternum
C. Ribs
D. Scapula
   1. Supraspinous fossa
   2. Acromial spine
   3. Infraspinous fossa
E. Humerus
   4. Proximal head
   5. Deltoid tuberosity
   6. Distal head
   7. Trochlea
   8. Lateral epicondyle
   9. Medial epicondyle
   10. Radial fossa

F. Radius
   11. Radial tuberosity
   12. Styloid process
G. Ulna
   13. Olecranon process
H. Carpal bones
I. Metacarpal bones
J. Phalanges

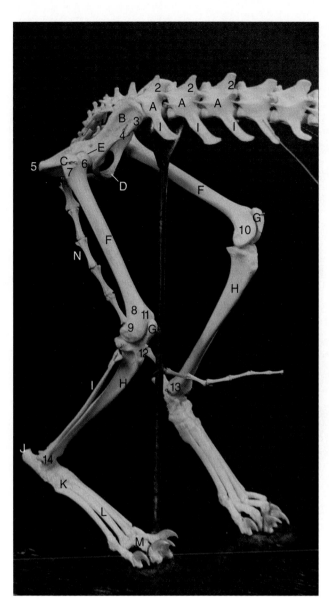

Figure 4-5
Cat Skeleton, Right Lateral Aspect

A. Lumbar vertebra
    1. Transverse process
    2. Spinous process
B. Ilium
    3. Cranial ventral iliac spine
    4. Caudal ventral iliac spine
C. Ischium
    5. Ischial tuberosity
D. Pubis
E. Acetabulum
F. Femur
    6. Proximal head
    7. Greater trochanter
    8. Distal head
    9. Lateral condyle
    10. Medial condyle
    11. Trochlea
G. Patella
H. Tibia
    12. Tibial tuberosity
    13. Medial malleolus
I. Fibula
    14. Lateral malleolus
J. Calcaneus
K. Tarsal bones
L. Metatarsal bones
M. Phalanges
N. Caudal vertebrae

Figure 4-6
**Superficial Anatomy of
Cat Head and Neck,
Left Lateral View**
1. Vibrissal barrels for
   sensory hairs (whiskers)
2. Tongue
3. Buccinator muscle
4. Diagastric muscle
5. Temporalis muscle
6. Masseter muscle
7. Dorsal buccal branch of
   facial (VII) nerve
8. Ventral buccal branch of
   facial (VII) nerve
9. Parotid duct
10. Parotid gland
11. Submaxillary gland
12. Lymph node
13. External jugular vein
14. Transverse jugular vein
15. Anterior facial vein
16. Posterior facial vein
17. Sternohyoid muscle
18. Sternothyroid muscle
19. Cleidomastoid muscle
20. Sternomastoid muscle
21. Clavotrapezius muscle
22. Clavobrachialis muscle
23. Acromiotrapezius muscle

Figure 4-7
Superficial Anatomy of Cat Head and Neck, Ventral Aspect
1. Body of mandible
2. Digastric muscle
3. Mylohyoid muscle
4. Buccinator muscle
5. Masseter muscle
6. Dorsal branch of facial (VII) nerve
7. Ventral branch of facial (VII) nerve
8. Lymph node
9. Submaxillary gland
10. Anterior facial vein
11. Posterior facial vein
12. Transverse jugular vein
13. External jugular vein
14. Larynx
15. Trachea
16. Sternohyoid muscle
17. Sternothyroid muscle (unavoidably damaged on animal's right side during vascular perfusion)
18. Cleidomastoid muscle
19. Sternomastoid muscle
20. Clavotrapezius muscle
21. Clavobrachialis muscle
22. Pectoantebrachialis muscle
23. Sternum

Figure 4-8
Deep Anatomy of Cat Head and Neck, Left Ventrolateral Aspect

1. Lower canine tooth
2. Upper canine tooth
3. Upper premolar tooth
4. Lower premolar tooth
5. Body of mandible
6. Digastric muscle
7. Mylohyoid muscle
8. Temporalis muscle
9. Masseter muscle
10. Dorsal branch of facial (VII) nerve
11. Ventral branch of facial (VII) nerve
12. Parotid duct
13. Cutaneous branch of facial (VII) nerve
14. Platysma muscle (reflected)
15. Lymph node
16. Sternohyoid muscle
17. Sternothyroid muscle (reflected)
18. Sternomastoid muscle
19. Omohyoid muscle
20. 4th cervical nerve
21. 5th cervical nerve
22. Jugular vein
23. Subclavian vein
24. Musculocutaneous nerve
25. Radial nerve
26. Median nerve
27. Ulnar nerve
28. Thoracic nerve
29. Ventral thoracic nerve (cut)
30. Axillary nerve

Figure 4-9
Deep Anatomy of Cat Head and Neck, Oral Cavity with Mandible Removed
1. Upper canine tooth
2. Upper premolar tooth
3. Upper molar tooth
4. Hard palate with palatine rugae
5. Soft palate
6. Tongue
7. Foliate papillae
8. Isthmus of Fauces
9. Epiglottis
10. Palatine tonsil
11. Larynx
12. Thyroid gland (reflected)
13. Trachea
14. External jugular vein
15. Carotid artery
16. Esophagus
17. Lymph node

Figure 4-10
Superficial Muscles of the Cat
Thoracic Limb, Ventral Aspect

1. Clavobrachialis muscle
2. Pectoantebrachialis muscle
3. Pectoralis major muscle
4. Pectoralis minor muscle
5. Latissimus dorsi muscle
6. Epitrochlearis muscle
7. Flexor carpi ulnaris muscle
8. Palmaris longus muscle
9. Flexor carpi radialis muscle
10. Pronator teres muscle
11. Extensor carpi radialis muscle
12. Brachioradialis muscle (cut)
13. Cephalic vein
14. Antebrachial fascia
15. Ulnar nerve
16. Olecranon process of ulna
17. Flexor retinaculum (transverse carpal ligament)

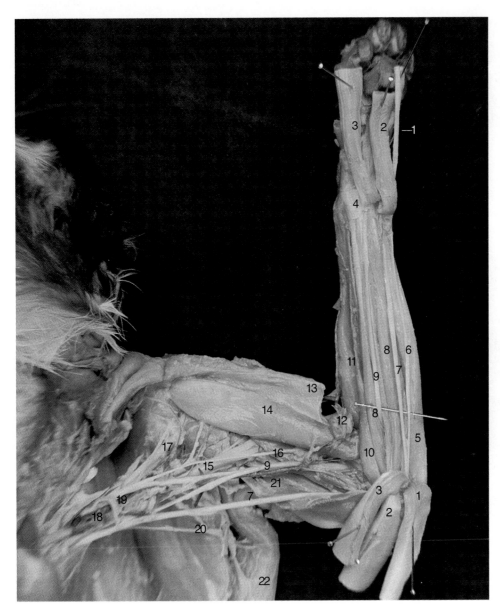

Figure 4-11
Deep Muscles of the Cat
Left Thoracic Limb,
Ventral Aspect

1. Flexor carpi ulnaris muscle (cut and reflected)
2. Palmaris longus muscle (cut and reflected)
3. Flexor carpi radialis muscle (cut and reflected)
4. Flexor retinaculum
5. Extensor carpi ulnaris
6. Cutaneous branch of ulnar nerve
7. Ulnar nerve
8. Flexor digitorum profundus
9. Median nerve
10. Pronator teres muscle
11. Extensor carpi radialis muscle
12. Brachioradialis muscle (cut)
13. Clavobrachialis muscle (cut and reflected)
14. Biceps brachii muscle
15. Radial nerve
16. Musculocutaneous nerve
17. Axillary nerve
18. Subclavian vein
19. Ventral thoracic nerve (cut)
20. Thoracic nerve
21. Triceps brachii muscle
22. Latissimus dorsi muscle

Figure 4-12
Superficial Muscles of the Cat Left Thoracic Limb, Dorsal Aspect

1. Flexor carpi ulnaris muscle
2. Extensor carpi ulnaris muscle
3. Extensor carpi digitorum lateralis muscle
4. Extensor pollicis brevis muscle
5. Extensor digitorum communis muscle
6. Extensor carpi radialis muscle
7. Brachioradialis muscle
8. Antebrachial fascia
9. Cephalic vein
10. Extensor retinaculum (dorsal carpal ligament)
11. Triceps brachii muscle (lateral head)
12. Triceps brachii muscle (long head)
13. Anconeus muscle
14. Brachialis muscle
15. Clavobrachialis muscle
16. Acromiodeltoid muscle
17. Spinodeltoid muscle
18. Acromiotrapezius muscle
19. Latissimus dorsi muscle
20. Levator scapulae ventralis

Figure 4-13
Deep Muscles of the Cat Left Thoracic Limb, Dorsal Aspect

1. Extensor carpi ulnaris muscle (cut)
2. Extensor digitorum lateralis muscle (cut)
3. Extensor digitorum communis muscle (cut)
4. Extensor indicis proprius muscle
5. Extensor pollicis brevis muscle
6. Extensor carpi radialis muscle
7. Brachioradialis muscle
8. Radial nerve
9. Cephalic vein
10. Extensor retinaculum (dorsal carpal ligament)
11. Extensor digiti minimi tendon
12. Extensor digitorum tendons
13. Extensor indicis tendon
14. Brachioradialis muscle
15. Median nerve
16. Ulnar nerve
17. Triceps brachii muscle (medial head)
18. Triceps brachii muscle (long head)
19. Triceps brachii muscle (lateral head, cut)
20. Anconeus muscle
21. Posterior interosseous nerve
22. Clavobrachialis muscle
23. Acromiodeltoid muscle
24. Spinodeltoid muscle
25. Latissimus dorsi muscle

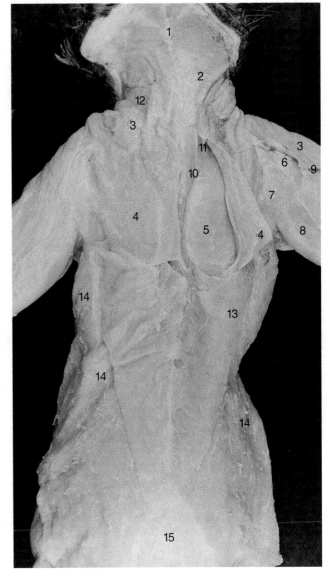

Figure 4-14
Superficial Muscles of the Cat Neck and Back

1. Nuchal ligament
2. Clavotrapezius muscle
3. Clavobrachialis muscle
4. Acromiotrapezius muscle (cut and reflected on right)
5. Supraspinatus muscle
6. Acromiodeltoid muscle
7. Spinodeltoid muscle
8. Triceps brachii muscle (long head)
9. Cephalic vein
10. Rhomboideus minor muscle
11. Rhomboideus capitis muscle (occipito-scapularis muscle)
12. Splenius capitis muscle
13. Spinotrapezius muscle
14. Latissimus dorsi muscle
15. Lumbodorsal fascia

Figure 4-15
Deep Muscles of the Cat Neck and Back

1. Nuchal ligament
2. Clavotrapezius muscle (reflected on left)
3. Acromiotrapezius muscle (cut, removed altogether on left)
4. Supraspinatus muscle
5. Infraspinatus muscle
6. Triceps brachii muscle (long head)
7. Triceps brachii muscle (lateral head)
8. Acromiodeltoid muscle
9. Clavobrachialis muscle
10. Rhomboideus capitis muscle
11. Splenius capitis muscle
12. Rhomboideus minor muscle
13. Rhomboideus major muscle
14. Spinotrapezius muscle
15. Latissimus dorsi muscle (reflected on left, partially removed on right)
16. Multifidus muscle
17. Spinalis muscle
18. Longissimus muscle
19. Iliocostalis muscle
20. Lumbodorsal fascia (largely removed)

A

B

Figure 4-16
Deep Muscles of the Back of the Cat

1. Spinotrapezius muscle
2. Latissimus dorsi muscle (cut and rolled on right)
3. Lumbodorsal fascia
4. Multifidus muscle
5. Spinalis muscle
6. Longissimus muscle
7. Iliocostalis muscle
8. Rib
9. Dorsal ramus of spinal nerve
10. External oblique muscle
11. External intercostal muscle
12. Internal intercostal muscle

Figure 4-17
**Superficial Muscles of
the Cat Left Hind Limb,
Dorsal Aspect**

1. Lumbodorsal fascia
2. Sartorius muscle
3. Tensor fascia latae
   muscle
4. Iliotibial band
5. Gluteus medius muscle
6. Gluteus maximus muscle
7. Caudofemoralis muscle
8. Biceps femoris muscle
9. Semitendinosus muscle
10. Semimembranosus
    muscle
11. Gastrocnemius muscle
12. Soleus muscle
13. Achilles tendon
14. Calcaneal tuberosity
15. Flexor hallucis longus
    muscle
16. Peroneus longus muscle
17. Extensor digitorum
    longus muscle
18. Tibialis anterior muscle

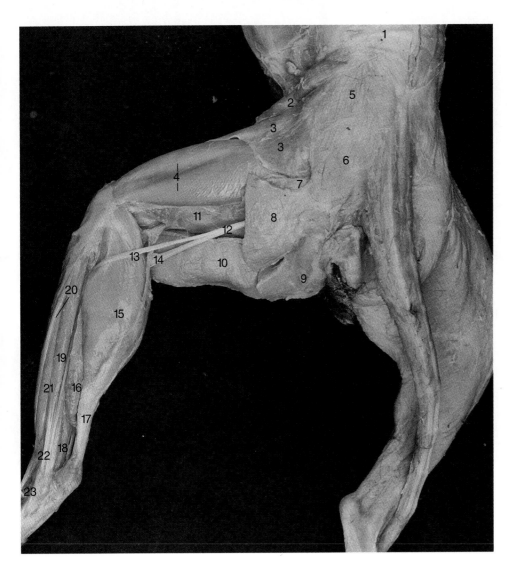

Figure 4-18
Deep Muscles of the Cat Left Hind Limb, Dorsal Aspect
1. Lumbodorsal fascia
2. Sartorius muscle
3. Tensor fascia latae muscle
4. Vastus lateralis muscle
5. Gluteus medius muscle (under fascia)
6. Gluteus maximus muscle (under fascia)
7. Caudofemoralis muscle
8. Biceps femoris muscle (cut)
9. Semitendinosus muscle (cut)
10. Semimembranosus muscle
11. Adductor femoris muscle
12. Sciatic nerve
13. Common peroneal division of sciatic nerve
14. Tibial division of sciatic nerve
15. Gastrocnemius muscle
16. Soleus muscle
17. Achilles tendon
18. Flexor hallucis longus muscle
19. Peroneus longus muscle
20. Tibialis anterior muscle
21. Extensor digitorum longus muscle
22. Proximal extensor retinaculum
23. Distal extensor retinaculum

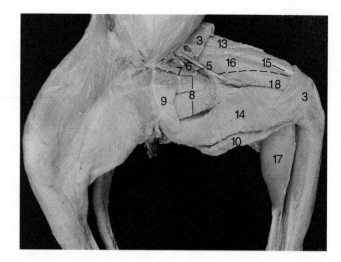

Figure 4-19
Superficial Muscles of the Cat Left Hind Limb, Medial Aspect

1. Rectus abdominis muscle
2. External oblique muscle
3. Sartorius muscle (cut)
4. Iliopsoas muscle (deep to blood vessels)
5. Femoral artery (a), vein (v), and nerve (n)
6. Pectineus muscle (deep to blood vessels)
7. Adductor longus muscle
8. Adductor femoris muscle
9. Gracilis muscle
10. Semitendinosus muscle
11. Greater saphenous vein
12. Branch of obturator nerve
13. Tensor fascia latae muscle
14. Semimembranosus muscle
15. Vastus lateralis muscle
16. Rectus femoris muscle
17. Gastrocnemius muscle
18. Vastus medialis muscle

Figure 4-20
Deep Muscles of the Cat Left Hind Limb, Medial Aspect

1. Sartorius muscle (cut)
2. Tensor fascia latae muscle
3. Vastus lateralis muscle
4. Rectus femoris muscle
5. Femoral artery (a), vein (v), and nerve (n)
6. Middle caudal femoral artery and vein
7. Pectineus muscle
8. Adductor longus muscle
9. Adductor femoris muscle
10. Gracilis muscle (cut)
11. Semimembranosus muscle
12. Semitendinosus muscle
13. Biceps femoris muscle
14. Gastrocnemius muscle (reflected)
15. Soleus muscle
16. Achilles tendon
17. Posterior tibial nerve
18. Flexor hallucis longus muscle
19. Flexor digitorum longus muscle
20. Tibialis posterior muscle
21. Tibia
22. Tibialis anterior muscle
23. Proximal extensor retinaculum
24. Vastus medialis muscle

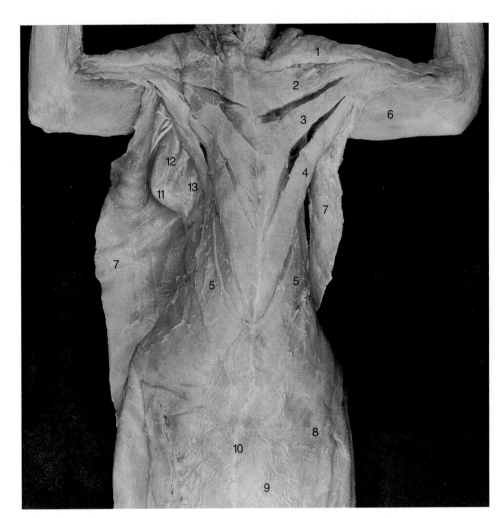

Figure 4-21
Superficial Muscles of the Cat Thorax, Ventral View

1. Clavobrachialis muscle
2. Pectoantebrachialis muscle
3. Pectoralis major muscle
4. Pectoralis minor muscle
5. Xiphihumeralis muscle
6. Epitrochlearis muscle
7. Latissimus dorsi muscle
8. External oblique muscle
9. Rectus abdominis muscle (deep to aponeurosis)
10. Linea alba
11. Inferior angle of scapula
12. Teres major muscle
13. Subscapularis muscle

Figure 4-22
Deep Muscles of the Cat Shoulder and Thorax, Right Ventral View

1. Latissimus dorsi muscle (reflected)
2. Scalenus muscles
   a. Anterior (continuous with transversus costarum)
   b. Medius
   c. Posterior
3. Axillary artery (a) and vein (v)
4. Radial nerve
5. External jugular vein
6. Internal jugular vein
7. Thoracodorsal nerve
8. Long thoracic nerve
9. Thoracoacromial blood vessels
10. Serratus ventralis muscle
11. Teres major muscle
12. Subscapularis muscle
13. Sternum
14. Ventral thoracic nerve

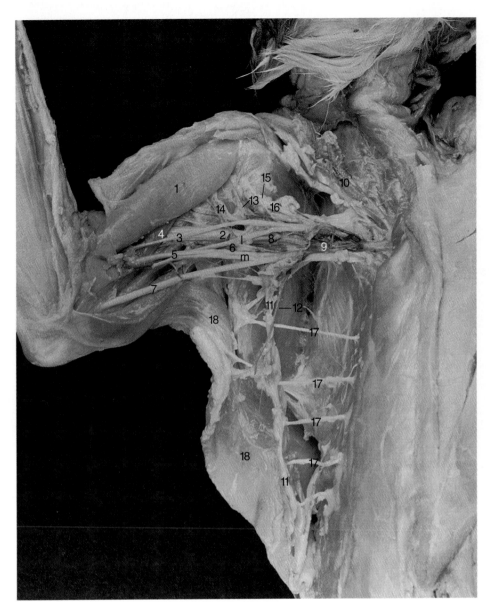

Figure 4-23
Brachial Plexus of the Cat,
Right Ventral Aspect
1. Biceps brachii muscle
2. Radial nerve
3. Musculocutaneous nerve
4. Coracobrachialis muscle
5. Median nerve
6. Lateral (l) and median (m) roots of the median nerve
7. Ulnar nerve
8. Axillary artery
9. Axillary vein
10. External jugular vein
11. Thoracodorsal nerve
12. Thoracodorsal artery
13. Thoracoacromial artery
14. Anterior circumflex humeral artery and axillary nerve
15. Caudal subscapular nerve
16. Proximal subscapular nerve
17. Dorsal rami of thoracic nerves
18. Latissimus dorsi muscle (reflected)

Figure 4-24
Thoracic Cavity of the Cat
1. Heart within
   pericardium
2. Thymus gland
3. Diaphragm
4. Lung, anterior lobe
5. Lung, middle lobe
6. Lung, posterior lobe
7. Ribs (cut)

Figure 4-25
**Major Veins of the Cat,
Neck and Thorax**

1. External jugular vein
2. Internal jugular vein
3. Common carotid artery (right)
4. Vagus nerve
5. Trachea
6. Transverse scapular vein
7. Subscapular vein
8. Thoracodorsal vein
9. Subclavian vein
10. Cephalic vein
11. Axillary vein
12. Latissimus dorsi muscle
13. Brachial vein
14. Median cubital vein
15. Innominate (brachiocephalic) vein
16. Anterior vena cava
17. Radial nerve
18. Median nerve
19. Ulnar nerve
20. Thoracodorsal nerve
21. Lymph node
22. Submaxillary gland
23. Parotid gland
24. Heart
25. Lung
26. Thymus gland
27. Anterior thoracic vein (cut) (internal mammary vein)
28. Long thoracic vein (cut)

Figure 4-26
Major Arteries of the Cat, Neck and Thorax

1. Common carotid artery
2. Vagus nerve
3. Vertebral artery
4. Transverse scapular artery
5. Axillary artery
6. Brachial artery
7. Thoraco-acromial artery (a) and nerve (n)
8. Musculocutaneous nerve
9. Median nerve
10. Radial nerve
11. Ulnar nerve
12. Trachea
13. Esophagus (displaced to animal's left from normal position posterior to trachea)
14. Phrenic nerve
15. Right subclavian artery
16. Innominate (brachiocephalic) artery
17. Left subclavian artery
18. Aortic arch
19. Anterior vena cava (cut)
20. Teres major muscle
21. Subscapularis muscle
22. Biceps brachii muscle
23. Triceps brachii muscle (long head)
24. Heart
25. Lung, anterior lobe
26. Lung, middle lobe
27. Lung, mediastinal lobe
28. Lung, posterior lobe
29. Right auricle
30. Diaphragm

Figure 4-27
Thorax of the Cat, Heart and Lungs Removed

1. Trachea
2. Esophagus
3. Aortic arch
4. Brachiocephalic artery
5. Right common carotid artery
6. Left common carotid artery
7. Vagus nerve
8. Sympathetic trunk
9. Left subclavian artery
10. Phrenic nerve
11. Vertebral artery
12. Subclavian artery
13. Thyrocervical artery
14. Internal mammary artery
15. Right and left primary bronchi
16. Inferior vena cava
17. Diaphragm
18. Rib
19. Transverse scapular artery
20. Subscapular artery (cut)

A

B

Figure 4-28
Veins, Arteries, and Nerves of the Cat Neck and Thorax
A, Veins Removed on Cat's Left Side, Heart Reflected to Right
B, Arteries, Veins, and Thoracic Viscera Removed

1. Larynx
2. Thyroid gland (reflected)
3. Common carotid artery
4. Vagus nerve
5. Sympathetic trunk (In **A**, two pins have been placed along sympathetic trunk. Upper pin head is just caudal to swelling of sympathetic trunk, the superior cervical ganglion. Lower transverse pin is just proximal to similar swelling, the middle cervical ganglion.)
6. Phrenic nerve
7. Aorta

8. Spinal accessory nerve (XI)
9. Spinal nerves IV, V, and VI
10. Brachial plexus
11. Lymph node (reflected and pinned)
12. Soft palate (cut)
13. Eustachian tubes (hidden behind reflected tissue of soft palate)
14. Epiglottis
15. Internal jugular vein
16. External jugular vein
17. Subscapular vein
18. Brachial vein
19. Axillary vein
20. Subclavian vein

21. Innominate (brachiocephalic) vein
22. Anterior vena cava
23. Azygous vein (cut)
24. Heart (reflected to cat's right)
25. Right auricle
26. Left auricle
27. Diaphragm
28. Esophagus
29. Trachea
30. Radial nerve
31. Musculocutaneous nerve
32. Median nerve
33. Ulnar nerve
34. Caudal subscapular nerve
35. Axillary nerve

Figure 4-29
Superficial Muscles of the Cat,
Abdomen and Thorax

1. Clavobrachialis muscle
2. Pectoantebrachialis muscle
3. Pectoralis major muscle
4. Pectoralis minor muscle
5. Xiphihumeralis muscle (removed on right)
6. Serratus anterior muscle
7. Latissimus dorsi muscle (cut to reveal underlying muscles)
8. Epitrochlearis muscle
9. External oblique muscle (partially reflected)
10. Internal oblique muscle (partially reflected)
11. Transversalis abdominis muscle
12. Peritoneum
13. Rectus abdominis muscle
14. Linea alba

A

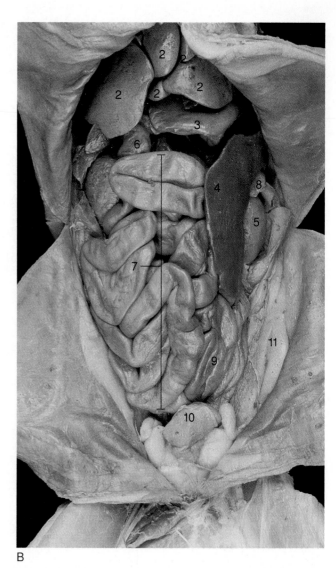

B

Figure 4-30
Abdominal Viscera of Cat with (A) Greater Omentum Intact and (B) Greater Omentum Removed

1. Greater omentum
2. Lobes of the liver
   R. Right lateral lobe
   M. Right medial lobe
   Q. Quadrate lobe
   N. Left medial lobe
   L. Left lateral lobe

3. Stomach (greater curvature)
4. Spleen
5. Kidney
6. Small intestine (duodenum)
7. Small intestine (jejuneum and ileum)
8. Pancreas

9. Large intestine (descending colon)
10. Urinary bladder
11. Abdominal fat

Figure 4-31
**Abdominal Viscera of
the Cat, Mesentery**
  1. Small intestine
  2. Mesentery
  3. Mesenteric artery
  4. Mesenteric vein
  5. Lymph vessel
  6. Urinary bladder
  7. Uterus
  8. Rectum
  9. Abdominal fat

A

B

Figure 4-32
Urogenital System of the Female Cat (A) Nonpregnant and (B) Pregnant

1. Liver
2. Stomach (pylorus)
3. Small intestine
4. Kidney
5. Ureter
6. Abdominal aorta
7. Common iliac artery
8. Caudal (median sacral) artery
9. Renal artery
10. Ovarian artery
11. Ovary
12. Urinary bladder (reflected and pinned)
13. Uterus
14. Uterine horn (in **B**, left horn contains two fetuses; right horn, three fetuses)
15. Rectum (cut in **A**)
16. External iliac artery and vein
17. Femoral triangle (containing femoral nerve, artery, and vein)
18. Ovarian vein
19. Iliolumbar vein
20. Abdominal vena cava (split into two parallel vessels in **A**)
21. Iliolumbar artery
22. Pancreas
23. Spleen
24. Adrenal gland
25. Hepatic portal vein (cut)
26. Fetus
27. Placenta
28. Left gastroepiploic vein
29. Right gastroepiploic vein

Figure 4-33
Urogenital System of the Male Cat
1. Liver
2. Stomach
3. Small intestine (duodenum, cut)
4. Kidney
5. Ureter
6. Abdominal aorta
7. Abdominal vena cava
8. Renal artery
9. Internal spermatic artery
10. Spermatic vein
11. Testis
12. Epididymis
13. Urinary bladder (reflected)
14. Vas deferens in spermatic cord
15. Urethra
16. Prostate gland
17. Bulbourethral (Cowper's) gland
18. Penis
19. Ligament of cremaster muscle
20. External inguinal ring
21. Femoral triangle
22. Rectum (cut)
23. Lumbar nerve (medial branch)
24. Umbilical (allantoic) artery
25. Spleen
26. Pancreas
27. Adrenal gland

A

B

Figure 4-34
Major (A) Veins and (B) Arteries of the Cat Abdominopelvic Wall

1. Kidney
2. Ureter (cut and largely removed)
3. Abdominal vena cava (removed in **B**)
4. Abdominal aorta (cut and removed in **A**)
5. Psoas muscle
6. Celiac artery (cut and removed)
7. Superior mesenteric artery (cut and removed)
8. Renal vein

9. Renal artery
10. Inferior mesenteric artery (cut and removed)
11. Iliolumbar vein
12. Iliolumbar artery
13. Common iliac vein
14. External iliac artery (no common iliac artery in cats)
15. External iliac vein
16. Internal iliac (hypogastric) artery
17. Internal iliac (hypogastric) vein

18. Femoral vein
19. Femoral artery
20. Deep femoral vein
21. Deep femoral artery
22. Caudal vein
23. Median sacral (caudal) artery
24. Rectum (cut)
25. Urinary bladder (reflected and pinned)

Figure 4-35
Nerves and Vessels of the Posterior Abdominopelvic Wall of the Cat

1. Abdominal aorta
2. Celiac artery (pinned)
3. Superior mesenteric artery (pinned)
4. Crus of diaphragm
5. Right adrenolumbar (phrenicoabdominal) artery (cut)
6. Adrenal gland
7. Renal vein
8. Renal artery
9. Ureter (cut)
10. Kidney
11. Inferior mesenteric artery
12. Iliolumbar artery
13. Psoas muscle
14. Femoral nerve
15. External iliac artery
16. Internal iliac artery
17. External iliac vein
18. Deep femoral artery and vein
19. Femoral artery
20. Femoral vein
21. Spermatic artery
22. Rectum (cut)
23. Urethra (cut and urinary bladder removed)
24. Prostate gland
25. Testis
26. Penis
27. Genitofemoral nerve
28. Distribution of sympathetic trunk (pinned out bilaterally)
29. Celiac ganglion
30. Superior mesenteric ganglion
31. Left adrenolumbar artery and vein

Figure 4-36
Superficial Muscles of the
Fetal Pig, Left Lateral View

1. Clavotrapezius muscle
2. Clavobrachialis muscle
3. Acromiodeltoid muscle
4. Spinodeltoid muscle
5. Triceps brachii muscle
6. Spinotrapezius muscle (cut)
7. Latissimus dorsi muscle
8. External oblique muscle (cut)
9. Serratus anterior muscle
10. Internal oblique muscle
11. Tensor fascia latae muscle (split)
12. Vastus lateral muscle (under pin)
13. Gluteus medius muscle
14. Gluteus maximus muscle
15. Biceps femoris muscle
16. Semitendinosus muscle
17. Semimembranosus muscle
18. Testis
19. Umbilical cord

A

B

Figure 4-37
Superficial Structures of the Neck, Shoulder, and Thoracic Limb of the Fetal Pig, Left Lateral View

1. Brachioradialis muscle
2. Extensor carpi radialis muscle
3. Extensor digitorum communis muscle
4. Extensor digitorum lateralis muscle
5. Extensor carpi ulnaris muscle
6. Masseter muscle
7. Submaxillary gland
8. Lymph node
9. Parotid gland
10. Salivary duct
11. External jugular vein
12. Clavotrapezius muscle
13. Clavobrachialis muscle
14. Acromiodeltoid muscle
15. Spinodeltoid muscle
16. Spinotrapezius muscle (cut)
17. Triceps brachii muscle (long head)
18. Triceps brachii muscle (lateral head)
19. Splenius capitis muscle
20. Rhomboideus capitis muscle
21. Latissimus dorsi muscle
22. Sternomastoid muscle

Figure 4-38
Superficial Muscles of the Hind Limb of the Fetal Pig, Left Lateral View

1. Lumbodorsal fascia
2. External oblique muscle (reflected)
3. Internal oblique muscle
4. Tensor fascia latae muscle (split)
5. Vastus lateralis muscle (under pin)
6. Gluteus medius muscle
7. Gluteus maximus muscle
8. Biceps femoris muscle
9. Semitendinosus muscle
10. Semimembranosus muscle
11. Testis
12. Gastrocnemius muscle
13. Soleus muscle
14. Achilles tendon
15. Flexor hallucis longus muscle
16. Tibialis anterior muscle

Figure 4-39
Superficial Anatomy of the Fetal Pig Neck and Shoulders, Ventral Aspect
1. Mylohyoid muscle
2. Sternohyoid muscle
3. Larynx
4. Trachea
5. Sternomastoid muscle
6. External jugular vein
7. Lymph node
8. Submaxillary gland
9. Masseter muscle
10. Clavotrapezius muscle
11. Acromiodeltoid muscle
12. Clavobrachialis muscle
13. Pectoralis major muscle
14. Sternum

Figure 4-40
**Deep Anatomy of the Fetal
Pig, Neck and Thorax**

1. Larynx
2. Trachea
3. Thyroid gland
4. Common carotid artery
5. Vagus nerve
6. Internal jugular vein
7. External jugular vein
    (pinned bilaterally)
8. Cephalic vein
9. Subclavian vein
10. Superior vena cava
11. Internal mammary vein
    (cut, laid on lung tissue)
12. Right auricle
13. Left auricle
14. Heart
15. Lung
16. Diaphragm

A

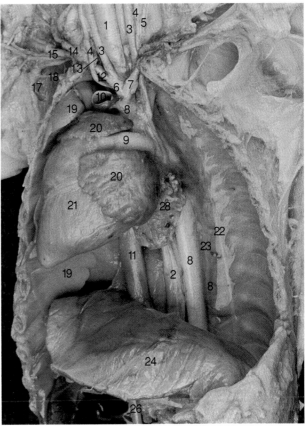

B

Figure 4-41
Arteries of the Neck and Thorax of the Fetal Pig, Left Lung Removed
A, Heart in Normal Position
B, Heart Reflected to Right

1. Trachea
2. Esophagus
3. Common carotid artery
4. Vagus nerve
5. Sympathetic trunk
6. Right innominate
   (brachiocephalic) artery
7. Left innominate (brachiocephalic)
   artery
8. Aorta
9. Ductus arteriosus

10. Superior vena cava (cut)
11. Inferior vena cava
12. Subclavian artery
13. Vertebral artery
14. Transverse scapular artery
15. Axillary artery
16. Radial nerve
17. Thoracodorsal nerve
18. Dorsal rami of thoracic nerves
19. Lung
20. Right and left auricles

21. Heart
22. Continuation of sympathetic trunk
23. Azygous vein
24. Diaphragm
25. Rib with costal artery and vein
26. Ductus venosus
27. Kidney
28. Hilum of left lung (with bronchi
    and blood vessels cut)

Figure 4-43
Abdominopelvic Cavity of the Fetal Pig, Male, Digestive Viscera Removed

1. Abdominal aorta
2. Abdominal vena cava
3. Renal artery
4. Renal vein
5. Kidney
6. Ureter
7. Spermatic artery
8. a. Vas deferens
   b. Vas deferens (in spermatic cord)
9. Testis
10. Epididymis
11. Penis
12. Rectum (cut)
13. Umbilical arteries
14. Umbilical vein
15. Ductus venosus (only remnants of liver remain)
16. Urinary bladder
17. Urethra
18. Prostate gland
19. Diaphragm
20. Heart
21. Lung
22. Pylorus of stomach (pin in antrum)

Figure 4-42
Thoracic and Abdominal Viscera of the Fetal Pig

1. Trachea
2. Thyroid gland
3. Thymus
4. Lung
5. Heart in pericardium
6. Mediastinal membrane
7. Diaphragm
8. Liver
9. Spleen
10. Ductus venosus (on pin)
11. Small intestine
12. Urinary bladder
13. Umbilical arteries
14. Umbilical vein
15. Penis
16. Urethra
17. Testis
18. Epididymis
19. Spermatic cord (contains spermatic artery and vas deferens, which curves to pass behind base of urinary bladder)

Figure 4-44
Abdominopelvic Cavity of the Fetal Pig, Female, Digestive Viscera Removed

1. Abdominal aorta
2. Abdominal vena cava
3. Kidney (behind intact peritoneum)
4. Ureter (behind intact peritoneum)
5. Ovarian artery
6. Ovary
7. Uterus
8. Uterine horn
9. Umbilical arteries
10. Umbilical vein (lying on pin)
11. Ductus venosus
12. Urinary bladder (reflected and pinned)
13. Sigmoid colon
14. Suspensory ligament of ovary
15. Diaphragm
16. Heart
17. Lung
18. Mediastinal membrane

Figure 4-45
Deep Anatomy of the Abdominopelvic Cavity of the Fetal Pig, Abdominal Viscera Removed, Female

1. Abdominal aorta
2. Abdominal vena cava
3. Renal vein
4. Ureter
5. Kidney (left kidney behind peritoneum)
6. Adrenal gland
7. Suspensory ligament of ovary
8. External iliac artery
9. Internal iliac artery
10. Median sacral (caudal) artery
11. Rectum (cut)
12. Ovary
13. Uterine horn
14. Urinary bladder (reflected)
15. Urethra
16. Umbilical arteries
17. Umbilical vein
18. Ductus venosus
19. Posterior (inferior) mesenteric artery
20. Colic artery (pinned to kidney for clarity due to missing colon)
21. Superior hemorrhoidal artery
22. Remnant of small intestine (duodenum)
23. Diaphragm

Figure 4-46
**General Anatomy of the Male Rat,
Abdominal Cavity Exposed, Ventral View**

1. Thorax
2. Abdomen
3. External oblique muscle (reflected and pinned)
4. Internal oblique muscle (lying on pin)
5. Transversus abdominis
6. Rectus abdominis
7. Peritoneum
8. Inferior epigastric artery
9. Liver
10. Spleen
11. Kidney
12. Rectum
13. Abdominal fat (small intestine not visible in this photograph)
14. Testis
15. Penis
16. Sternum (xiphoid process)

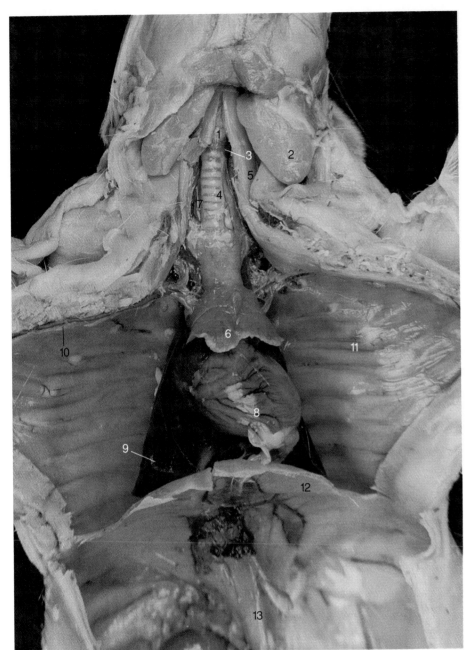

Figure 4-47
Deep Anatomy of the Rat,
Neck and Thorax
1. Larynx
2. Salivary gland
3. Thyroid gland
4. Trachea
5. Sternohyoid muscle
   (unavoidably damaged on
   animal's right side during
   vascular perfusion)
6. Thymus
7. Common carotid artery
8. Heart
9. Lung
10. Internal mammary vein
11. Rib and intercostal artery and
    vein
12. Diaphragm
13. Crus of diaphragm

Figure 4-48
Abdominopelvic Cavity of the Male Rat

1. Sternum (xiphoid process)
2. Stomach
3. Liver
4. Small intestine (duodenum)
5. Pancreas
6. Spleen
7. Kidney
8. Small intestine (jejuneum and ileum)
9. Large intestine (cecum)
10. Rectum
11. Abdominal fat
12. Urinary bladder
13. Rectus abdominis muscle (cut)
14. Testis in scrotum
15. Epididymis
16. Penis
17. Seminal vesicle
18. Cremasteric fascia

Figure 4-49
Abdominopelvic Cavity of the Rat, Male, Digestive Viscera Removed
1. Sternum (xiphoid process)
2. Abdominal aorta
3. Abdominal vena cava
4. Renal artery
5. Renal vein
6. Kidney
7. Adrenal gland
8. Ureter (lying on pin)
9. Spermatic artery (lying on pin)
10. Lumbar nerve (medial branch, extended for clarity)
11. Iliolumbar artery and vein
12. Urinary bladder
13. Seminal vesicle
14. Common iliac artery
15. Median sacral (caudal) artery
16. Rectum (cut)
17. Penis
18. Psoas muscle
19. Diaphragm
20. Crus of diaphragm

Figure 4-50
Abdominopelvic Cavity of the Rat, Female,
Digestive Viscera Removed
  1. Abdominal aorta
  2. Abdominal vena cava
  3. Renal artery
  4. Renal vein
  5. Ureter (lying on pin)
  6. Iliolumbar artery
  7. Iliolumbar vein
  8. Rectum (cut)
  9. Ovary
 10. Uterus
 11. Uterine horn
 12. Urinary bladder
 13. Abdominal fat
 14. Ovarian artery and vein
 15. Crus of diaphragm
 16. Kidney
 17. Adrenal gland

Reference Tables

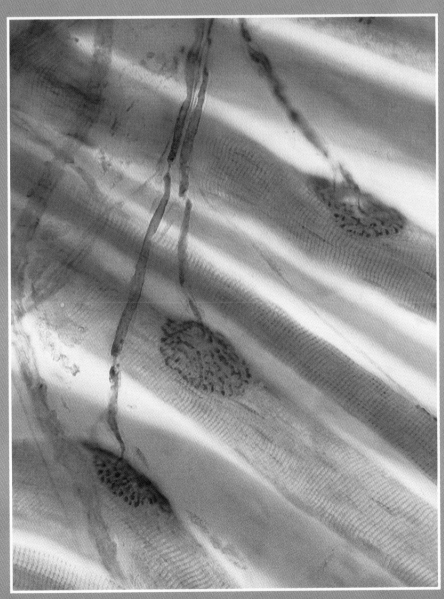

Innervation of Skeletal Muscle: Motor Endplate

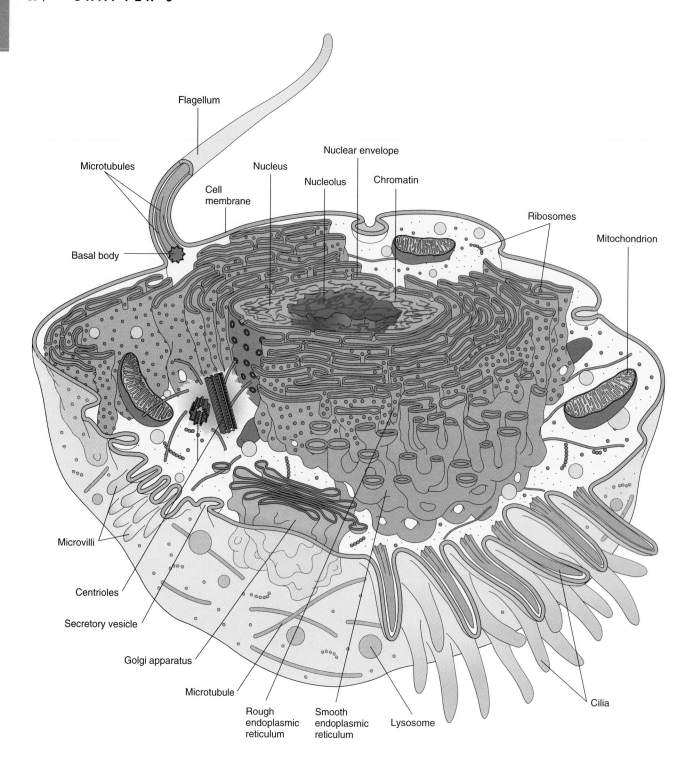

Figure 5-1
Generalized illustration of a cell.

TABLE 5.1   Structure and Function of Some Cellular Components

STRUCTURE	DESCRIPTION AND FUNCTION
MEMBRANOUS	
Plasma membrane	Composed mainly of phospholipid bilayer with globular proteins floating dynamically on, in, and through it. Separates living cell contents from nonliving environment. Maintains cellular integrity. Embedded molecules serve as identifying cell markers (antigens), receptor molecules for hormones and related substances, signal transducers, selective ion channels, and transporter mechanisms.
Endoplasmic reticulum	Complex of membranous canals, sacs, and vesicles. Transports material within the cell; provides attachment for ribosomes; contributes to synthesis of lipids, steroids, and some carbohydrates used to form glycoproteins.
Golgi apparatus	Flattened membranous sacs. Synthesizes and packages carbohydrates and glycoproteins.
Lysosomes	Small membranous sacs. Contains enzymes used in intracellular digestion.
Peroxisomes	Small membranous vesicles. Contains peroxidase enzymes used in breakdown of complex toxins and other organic molecules.
Mitochondria	Small membranous sacs with complex internal structure and separate DNA. Contains enzymes of Krebs cycle; central to carbohydrate metabolism and synthesis of ATP.
Nucleus	Nuclear contents, notably DNA, separated from cytoplasm by porous nuclear envelope.
NONMEMBRANOUS	
Ribosomes	Small structures composed of two parts containing protein and RNA molecules. Often associated with endoplasmic reticulum. Synthesizes proteins under instructions of messenger RNA triplet code.
Centrosome	Double structure composed of two, short, rod-like centrioles. Important in distribution of chromosomes during cell division and in formation of cilia.
Microfilaments and microtubules	Composed of protein complexes. Acts as cytoskeletal framework. Functions in whole-cell and local membrane movements, cellular elasticity, and formation of cellular extensions (e.g., microvilli).
Cilia and flagella	Movable membranous extensions. Important in movement of fluid environment over stationary cell surface (cilia) and cell itself (flagellum of sperm cell).
Nucleolus	Dense object composed of protein and RNA molecules. Essential in ribosome formation.

TABLE 5.2   Some Membrane Transport Processes

PROCESS	DESCRIPTION
PHYSICAL PROCESSES: DO NOT REQUIRE LOCAL EXPENDITURE OF METABOLIC ENERGY	
Bulk flow	Movement of substances from higher pressures toward lower pressures. Examples: movement of gases in and out of ventilatory tree during breathing, movement of blood through arteries and veins due to pumping action of heart.
Diffusion	Movement of ions or molecules from higher concentrations toward lower concentrations due to random molecular collisions. Examples: movement of sodium and potassium ions and glucose molecules in extracellular fluid.
Filtration	Bulk flow through a semipermeable membrane. Example: movement of fluid and small molecules through kidney capillary walls due to hydrostatic pressure.
Dialysis	Diffusion of solute molecules through a semipermeable membrane. Example: passage of lipid-soluble substances, such as steroid molecules, through cell membrane.
Osmosis	Diffusion of water down *its* concentration gradient through a semipermeable membrane. Osmosis generally operates *against* concentration gradient of solute(s) to which the membrane is *im*permeable. Example: net movement of extracellular fluid into the venous ends of capillaries under influence of *im*permeant plasma proteins.
Facilitated diffusion	Diffusion through an otherwise impermeable membrane by means of carrier molecules. Example: movement of glucose through muscle cell membranes (requires insulin to enhance action of facilitating carriers).
PHYSIOLOGICAL PROCESSES: REQUIRE LOCAL EXPENDITURE OF METABOLIC ENERGY	
Active transport	Carrier-mediated transport of ions or molecules through a living membrane via energy-requiring shape change of carrier molecule. Energy expenditure permits transport from lower to higher concentration. Examples: movement of sodium from inside to outside of resting nerve cells; transport of potassium and calcium from outside to inside cells, thereby causing high internal concentrations of these ions.
Phagocytosis and pinocytosis	Transport of large particles or fluid into a cell via engulfing action of membrane followed by pinching off to form an intracellular vesicle. Both are processes of endocytosis. Example: trapping of bacteria by white blood cells.
Exocytosis	Transport of substances out of a cell by fusion of internal vesicle with cell membrane and release of contents to the exterior. Examples: secretion of hormones and neurotransmitters, such as prolactin and acetylcholine.

TABLE 5.3   Terms for Bone Structure

TERM	DEFINITION
Epiphysis	Either rounded end of head of a long bone
Diaphysis	The shaft of a long bone
Anatomic neck	The epiphyseal growth plate
Surgical neck	The narrow part of a long bone, just past the head, where fracture is most likely
Ramus	A branch
Cornu	A horn
Hamulus	A hook
Lingula	A tongue
Foramen (pl. foramina)	A hole; an opening into or through a bone to permit passage of blood vessels, nerves, or ligaments
Fossa	A valley; a relatively deep pit or depression
Fovea	A relatively small pit or depression
Sulcus	A narrow valley
Meatus	A tunnel
Trochanter	A large, blunt, rounded process that serves as a site for muscle attachment
Tubercle	A small, blunt, rounded process that serves as a site for muscle attachment
Tuberosity	A large, rounded, often rough eminence or surface that serves as a site for muscle attachment
Condyle	A large, rounded process at the end of a bone, usually contributing to a joint
Epicondyle	A smaller, rounded process at the end of a bone, on top of a condyle, usually contributing to a joint
Trochlea	A pulley; a smooth notched surface often found at a joint
Facet	A face; a smooth, nearly flat surface at a joint
Fissure	A crack or cleft
Crest or crista	A narrow ridge
Spine	A pointed ridge
Fontanel	Specifically, six spaces between the cranial bones of the fetal and infant skull prior to closure of the sutures
Second and fifth intercostal spaces	Specifically refers to a place between the 1st and 2nd rib and a place between the 5th and 6th rib where the second and first heart sounds, respectively, can be heard especially well

TABLE 5.4   Bones of the Human Skeleton

PART OF THE BODY	NAMES OF BONES
AXIAL SKELETON (80 BONES TOTAL)	
Skull (28 bones)	
Cranium (8 bones)*	Frontal (1) Parietal (1 pair) Temporal (1 pair) Occipital (1) Sphenoid (1) Ethmoid (1)
Face (14 bones)	Lacrimal (1 pair) Nasal (1 pair) Palatine (1 pair) Inferior nasal conchae (turbinates) (1 pair) Vomer (1) Maxillae (1 pair) Zygomatic (malar) (1 pair) Mandible (1)
Middle ear (6 bones)	Malleus (1 pair) Incus (1 pair) Stapes (1 pair)
Hyoid bone (1)	
Spinal column (26 bones total)	Cervical vertebrae (7) Thoracic vertebrae (12) Lumbar vertebrae (5) Sacrum (4–5 fused into 1) Coccyx (4–5 fused into 1)
Sternum and ribs (25 bones total)	Sternum (1) True ribs (7 pairs) False ribs (5 pairs)
APPENDICULAR SKELETON (126 BONES TOTAL)	
Shoulder girdle and arm (64 bones total)	Clavicle (1 pair) Scapula (1 pair) Humerus (1 pair) Ulna (1 pair) Radius (1 pair) Carpals (8 pairs; navicular (scaphoid), lunate, triangular (triquetum), pisiform, greater multangular (trapezium), lesser multangular (trapezoid), capitate, hamate) Metacarpals (5 pairs) Phalanges (14 pairs)
Pelvic girdle and leg (62 bones total)	Os coxae (1 pair: 2 innominate bones each formed by fusion of ilium, ischium, and pubis) Femur (1 pair) Patella* (1 pair) Tibia (1 pair) Fibula (1 pair) Tarsals (7 pairs: Talus, calcaneus, navicular, medial cuneiform, intermediate cuneiform, lateral cuneiform, cuboid. Metatarsals (5 pairs) Phalanges (14 pairs)

*A variable number of rounded bones known as **sesamoid bones** (because of their supposed resemblance to sesame seeds) may appear in various tendons, especially those in the wrist, knee, ankle, and foot. Only two of them, the patellae, are commonly found. **Wormian bones** are found in variable numbers within the suture lines of the skull. While most are commonly smaller than the size of fingernails, some can be surprisingly large.

TABLE 5.5 — Comparison of Female and Male Skeletons

Differences between male and female skeletons are graded, not discrete. Female skeletons can have many masculine features, and vice versa. Nevertheless, there are trends, including those listed below. A typically masculine pelvis is called *android;* a typically feminine pelvis is called *gynecoid.* Many intermediate types exist.

PORTION OF SKELETON	FEMALE	MALE
GENERAL FORM	Bones lighter and thinner Muscle attachment sites smaller and smoother Joint surfaces relatively small	Bones heavier and thicker Muscle attachment sites larger and rougher Joint surfaces relatively large
PELVIS		
Pelvic cavity	Wider in all dimensions Shorter and roomier Pelvic outlet relatively large	Smaller in all dimensions Deeper Pelvic outlet usually obstructed
Sacrum	Short, wide, flat concavity more pronounced in a posterior direction; sacral promontory less pronounced	Long, narrow, with smooth concavity of sacral curvature; sacral promontory more pronounced
Coccyx	More movable and follows posterior direction of sacral curvature	Less movable
Pubic arch	Greater than a 90° angle	Less than a 90° angle
Ischial spine, ischial tuberosity, and anterior super iliac spine	Oriented outward and further apart	Oriented inward
Greater sciatic notch	Narrow	Wide

TABLE 5.6 — Extrinsic Muscles of the Eye

NAME	ORIGIN	INSERTION	ACTION	INNERVATION
Rectus superior	Tendinous ring of tissue at back of orbit which surrounds optic foramen	Top of eyeball	Rolls eye upward	Oculomotor
Rectus inferior		Bottom of eyeball	Rolls eye downward	Oculomotor
Rectus lateralis		Lateral side of eyeball	Rolls eye laterally	Abducens
Rectus medius		Medial side of eyeball	Rolls eye medially	Oculomotor
Obliquus superior		Top of eyeball under rectus superior, through trochlea	Prevents rotation of eyeball on axis; directs gaze down and laterally	Trochlear
Obliquus inferior	Maxilla at front of orbit	Lateral side of eyeball under rectus lateralis	Prevents rotation of eye on axis; directs gaze up and laterally	Oculomotor

TABLE 5.7   Facial Muscles

NAME	ORIGIN	INSERTION	ACTION	INNERVATION
Buccinator	Maxillary and mandibular alveolar processes	Into orbicularis oris at sides of mouth	Compresses cheek, retracts corner of mouth as in playing a brass musical instrument	Facial
Orbicularis oris	Maxillae, mandible, nasal septum	Fibers encircle mouth, insert on fascia	Puckering, shaping of mouth in speech	Facial
Orbicularis oculi	Maxillae, frontal bone	Fibers encircle orbit	Closes eye, assists in squinting	Facial
Epicranius (Occipitofrontalis)	Occipital bone	Skin around eyebrows and above nose	Moves scalp, elevates eyebrows	Facial
Zygomaticus major	Zygomatic bone	Into orbicularis oris at corners of mouth	Retracts and elevates corners of mouth as in smiling	Facial
Zygomaticus minor	Zygomatic bone	Into orbicularis oris of upper lip	Elevates upper lip, assists in smiling	Facial
Levator palpebrae superioris	Lesser wing of sphenoid	Skin of upper eyelid	Elevates upper eyelid	Oculomotor
Corrugator supercilii	Bridge of nose, orbicularis oculi	Skin of eyebrows	Depresses and adducts eyebrows; furrows forehead as in frowning	Facial

TABLE 5.8   Chewing Muscles

NAME	ORIGIN	INSERTION	ACTION	INNERVATION
Masseter	Zygomatic arch and maxilla	Lateral surface of mandible	Closes jaw	Trigeminal
Temporalis	Temporal bone	Coronoid process of mandible	Closes jaw	Trigeminal
Pterygoid (medial and lateral)	Pterygoid processes of sphenoid bone	Medial surface of mandible	Moves jaw from side to side; grates teeth for chewing	Trigeminal

TABLE 5.9 — Muscles of the Throat

NAME	ORIGIN	INSERTION	ACTION	INNERVATION
Digastric	Mastoid process of temporal bone	Mandible	Elevates hyoid bone; depresses and retracts mandible	Posterior portion: Facial Anterior portion: Mandibular branch of trigeminal
Mylohyoid	Mandible	Hyoid	Elevates floor of mouth when mandible is fixed; depresses mandible when hyoid is fixed	Mandibular division of trigeminal
Omohyoid	Superior border of scapula and tendon from clavicle	Hyoid	Depresses hyoid; stabilizes hyoid when opening mouth	C1–C3 via ansa hypoglossi
Sternohyoid	Manubrium of sternum; costal cartilage 1	Hyoid	Depresses hyoid; stabilizes hyoid when opening mouth	C1–C3 via ansa hypoglossi
Sternothyroid	Manubrium of sternum; costal cartilages 1 and 2	Thyroid cartilage	Depresses larynx; stabilizes larynx when opening mouth	Upper cervical nerves via ansa cervicalis and ansa hypoglossi

TABLE 5.10 — Muscles of the Tongue

NAME	ORIGIN	INSERTION	ACTION	INNERVATION
Intrinsic muscles: Longitudinal, vertical, and transverse	Within tongue	Within tongue	Change shape of tongue in speaking, chewing, licking	Hypoglossal
Genioglossus	Genu of mandible	Tongue	Depresses and protrudes tongue	Hypoglossal
Hyoglossus	Hyoid	Side of tongue	Depresses and retracts tongue	Hypoglossal
Styloglossus	Styloid process of temporal bone	Inferior and lateral aspect of tongue	Retracts tongue	Hypoglossal

NOTE: The three above-named muscles are **extrinsic muscles of the tongue**, so identified because their origins lie outside the muscular tongue itself.

TABLE 5.11   Muscles of the Pharynx and Palate

NAME	ORIGIN	INSERTION	ACTION	INNERVATION
Constrictor pharyngis inferior	Cricoid and thyroid cartilages	Median raphe of pharynx	Constricts lower pharynx during swallowing	Glossopharyngeal and vagus
Constrictor pharyngis medius	Greater and lesser cornu of hyoid	Median raphe of pharynx	Constricts middle pharynx during swallowing	Glossopharyngeal and vagus
Constrictor pharyngis superior	Middle pterygoid plate, mandible, floor of mouth	Median raphe of pharynx	Constricts upper pharynx during swallowing	Glossopharyngeal and vagus
Stylopharyngeus	Styloid process of temporal bone	Sides of pharynx; thyroid cartilage	Elevates and dilates pharynx	Glossopharyngeal
Palatopharyngeus	Soft palate	Pharynx	Narrows fauces; depresses palate; elevates pharynx	Glossopharyngeal and vagus
Palatoglossus	Soft palate	Tongue	Narrows fauces; elevates back of tongue	Pharyngeal plexus
Levator veli palatini	Temporal bone and cartilage of Eustachian tube	Soft palate	Elevates soft palate	Glossopharyngeal and vagus
Tensor veli palatini	Sphenoid bone and cartilage of Eustachian tube	Soft palate	Increases tension of soft palate; opens Eustachian tube as in yawning	Mandibular division of trigeminal

NOTE: The palatopharyngeus muscle and its mucous membrane covering form the clearly seen arch of the soft palate, from which hangs the uvula. Just anterior to this arch on each side is the palatoglossus muscle which, with its mucous membrane covering, forms the more lateral and less clearly seen glossopalatine arch. Between these two arches on each side is a fossa that houses the lymph node known as the palatine tonsil.

TABLE 5.12   Muscles That Move the Head

NAME	ORIGIN	INSERTION	ACTION	INNERVATION
Sternocleidomastoid	Sternum and clavicle	Mastoid process of temporal bone	Bows head, rotates head	Spinal accessory, C2–C3
Trapezius	Acromial process of clavicle and spine of scapula	Occipital bone, ligamentum nuchae, spines of 7th cervical and all thoracic vertebrae	Extends head, rotates head	Spinal accessory, C3–C4
Obliquus capitis inferior	Spinous process of axis	Transverse process of atlas	Rotates head	Branch of suboccipital
Splenius capitis	Ligamentum nuchae, spines of 7th cervical and top four thoracic vertebrae	Occipital bone and mastoid process of temporal bone	Extends head, rotates head	Middle and lower cervical spinal nerves
Semispinalis capitis	See MUSCLES OF THE VERTEBRAL COLUMN. The capitis division of this muscle inserts on the occipital bone. When the vertebrae serve as the origin and the occipital bone as the insertion, this muscle (bilaterally) extends the head or (unilaterally) draws the head toward the contracting side.			
Longissimus capitis	See MUSCLES OF THE VERTEBRAL COLUMN. The capitis division of this muscle inserts on the mastoid process of the temporal bone. When the vertebrae serve as the origin and the occipital bone as the insertion, this muscle (bilaterally) extends the head or (unilaterally) draws and rotates the head toward the contracting side.			

TABLE 5.13 Muscles That Move the Shoulder

NAME	ORIGIN	INSERTION	ACTION	INNERVATION
Trapezius	See MUSCLES THAT MOVE THE HEAD. If origin and insertion are reversed, this muscle causes elevation of shoulders, as in shrugging, by elevating clavicle and scapula.			
Pectoralis minor	Outer surface of third, fourth, and fifth ribs	Coracoid process of scapula	Depresses shoulder, rotates scapula forward and down; can assist in elevating ribs	Long thoracic
Serratus anterior	Outer surface of upper eight or nine ribs	Ventral surface of vertebral border of scapula	Rotates scapula forward and toward thoracic wall; can assist in elevating ribs	Spinal accessory, C3–C4
Rhomboideus major	Spines of second to fifth thoracic vertebrae	Vertebral border of scapula	Adducts scapula, rotates slightly upward	Dorsal scapular
Rhomboideus minor	Spines of seventh cervical and first thoracic vertebrae	Vertebral border of scapula	Adducts scapula	Dorsal scapular

NOTE: The **triangle of auscultation** is formed at the caudal medial border of the scapula by the edges of the latissimus dorsi, trapezius, and rhomboideus muscles.

TABLE 5.14 Muscles That Move the Upper Arm

NAME	ORIGIN	INSERTION	ACTION	INNERVATION
Pectoralis major	Clavicle, sternum, cartilages of second to sixth ribs	Crest and greater tubercle of humerus	Flexes and adducts arm	Anterior thoracic
Latissimus dorsi	Spinous processes of lower six thoracic and all lumbar vertebrae, sacral spine, iliac crest and lower four ribs	Intertubercular groove of humerus	Extends, adducts, rotates arm medially, draws shoulder down and back	Thoracodorsal
Deltoideus	Clavicle and acromion and spine of scapula	Deltoid tuberosity of humerus	Abducts arm	Axillary
Coracobrachialis	Coracoid process of scapula	Medial surface of humerus	Adducts arm; assists in flexion and medial rotation	Musculocutaneous
Teres major	Medial border of scapula	Just distal to lesser tubercle of humerus	Adducts, extends, rotates arm medially	Lower subscapular
Teres minor	Medial border of scapula	Greater tubercle of humerus	Rotates arm laterally	Axillary
Subscapularis	Subscapular fossa of scapula	Lesser tubercle of humerus	Extends and medially rotates arm	Subscapular C5, C6
Supraspinatus	Supraspinous fossa of scapula	Greater tubercle of humerus	Initiates abduction of arm	Suprascapular C5, C6
Infraspinatus	Infraspinous fossa of scapula	Greater tubercle of humerus	Extends and laterally rotates arm	Suprascapular C5, C6

NOTE: The **rotator cuff** is formed from the tendons of the last four muscles named above because together they form a cuff that binds the humerus into the shallow glenoid fossa. A rotator cuff injury involves damage to one or more of these muscles or their tendons.

NOTE: Alone, the deltoid cannot initiate the first 15° of abduction, which is a duty of the supraspinatus muscle and its innervation and which is separate from that of the deltoid. Differential assessment of peripheral nerve injury is possible by asking a patient to abduct the arm from anatomical position.

TABLE 5.15 — Muscles That Move the Lower Arm

NAME	ORIGIN	INSERTION	ACTION	INNERVATION

Biceps brachii	Long head:
	  Tuberosity above
	  glenoid cavity of
	  scapula
	Short head:
	  Coracoid process of
	  scapula
		Radial tuberosity	Flexes and supinates arm
			  and forearm
				Musculocutaneous

Brachialis	Anterior surface of
	  distal humerus
		Tuberosity and coronoid
		  process of ulna
			Flexes forearm	Musculocutaneous, radial,
				  and median

Brachioradialis	Supracondyloid ridge
	  of humerus
		Proximal to styloid
		  process of radius
			Flexes forearm	Radial

Triceps brachii	Long head:
	  Infraglenoid tuberosity
	  of scapula
	Lateral head:
	  Posterior surface of
	  humerus above radial
	  groove
	Medial head:
	  Posterior surface of
	  humerus below radial
	  groove
		Olecranon process of ulna	Extends forearm	Radial

Anconeus	Lateral epicondyle of
	  humerus
		Olecranon process and
		  proximal one-fourth
		  of ulna
			Extends forearm	Radial

Pronator teres	Medial epicondyle of
	  humerus, coronoid
	  process of ulna
		Middle third of lateral
		  surface of radius
			Pronates and flexes forearm	Median

Pronator quadratus	Distal shaft of ulna	Distal shaft of radius	Pronates forearm	Median

Supinator	Lateral epicondyle of
	  humerus, proximal
	  end of ulna
		Proximal third of radius	Supinates forearm	Median

TABLE 5.16   Muscles That Move the Wrist and Hand

NAME	ORIGIN	INSERTION	ACTION	INNERVATION
FLEXORS				
Flexor carpi ulnaris	Ulna; medial epicondyle of humerus	Fifth metacarpal; pisiform and hamate	Flexes and adducts wrist; flexes forearm	Ulnar
Palmaris longus	Medial epicondyle of humerus	Palmar fascia	Tenses palmar fascia; flexes wrist	Median
Flexor carpi radialis	Medial epicondyle of humerus	First and second metacarpals	Flexes and abducts wrist	Median
Flexor digitorum profundus	Ulna	Distal phalanges 2–5	Flexes fingers and wrist	Median and ulnar
Flexor digitorum superficialis	Medial epicondyle of radius	Middle phalanges 2–5	Flexes fingers and wrist	Median
Flexor pollicis longus	Radius	Distal phalanx of thumb	Flexes thumb and wrist	Median
EXTENSORS				
Extensor carpi ulnaris	Ulna; lateral epicondyle of humerus	Metacarpal 5	Extends hand; adducts little finger	Radial
Extensor digitorum	Lateral epicondyle of humerus	Phalanges 2–5	Extends fingers and wrist	Radial
Extensor carpi radialis brevis	Lateral epicondyle of humerus	Metacarpal 3	Extends and abducts wrist	Radial
Extensor carpi radialis longus	Lateral supracondylar ridge of humerus	Metacarpal 2	Extends and abducts wrist	Radial
Extensor indicis	Ulna	Phalanx 2	Extends forefinger and wrist	Radial
Abductor pollicis longus	Posterior ulna and radius; interosseous membrane	Metacarpal 1	Abducts and extends thumb and wrist	Radial
Extensor pollicis longus	Dorsal surface of ulna	Base of thumb, second phalanx	Extends end of thumb	Radial
Extensor pollicis brevis	Dorsal surface of radius	Dorsal surface of thumb, first phalanx	Extends and abducts thumb; abducts wrist	Posterior interosseous

NOTE: These last two muscles cross the lateral surface of the wrist to form the **anatomical snuff box**. Extend the thumb laterally to see this structure. The radial artery passes through the snuff box; the pulse can be felt there.

TABLE 5.17 — Muscles That Move the Chest Wall: Breathing

NOTE: These muscles are overlaid by the latissimus dorsi, trapezius, and the pectoralis, which are functionally part of the appendicular muscle division.

NAME	ORIGIN	INSERTION	ACTION	INNERVATION
External intercostals	Inferior border of rib	Superior border of rib	Draws adjacent ribs together	Intercostal
Internal intercostals	Inferior border of rib	Superior border of rib	Draws adjacent ribs together	Intercostal
Transversus thoracis	Lower one third of sternum	Costal cartilage of true ribs (except first rib)	Depresses ribs in exhalation	Intercostal
Diaphragm	Xiphoid process, costal cartilages of lowest six ribs, lumbar vertebrae	Central tendon	Depresses floor of thoracic cavity in inhalation	Phrenic
Sternocleidomastoid	See MUSCLES THAT MOVE THE HEAD. If head acts as origin, then this muscle acts to elevate sternum and rib cage.			
Scalenes	Transverse processes of second to seventh cervical vertebrae	First two ribs	Elevates ribs in inhalation	C5–C8
Levatores costarum	Transverse processes of seventh cervical and first eleven thoracic vertebrae	Angle of rib immediately below origin	Elevates ribs in inhalation	Intercostal

TABLE 5.18 — Muscles That Move the Abdominal Wall

NAME	ORIGIN	INSERTION	ACTION	INNERVATION
External oblique	Lower eight ribs	Iliac crest, linea alba	Compresses abdominal contents	Intercostals 8–12, iliohypogastric, ilioinguinal
Internal oblique	Iliac crest, inguinal ligament, lumbodorsal fascia	Costal cartilages of last three or four ribs	Compresses abdominal contents	Same as external oblique
Transversus abdominis	Iliac crest, inguinal ligament, lumbar fascia, costal cartilages of last six ribs	Xiphoid process, linea alba, pubis	Compresses abdominal contents	Intercostals 7–12, iliohypogastric, ilioinguinal
Rectus abdominis	Pubic crest, symphysis pubis	Xiphoid process, costal cartilages of fifth, six, and seventh ribs	Flexes trunk, compresses abdominal contents	Intercostals 7–12

TABLE 5.19   Muscles of the Pelvic Floor: The Pelvic Diaphragm

NAME	ORIGIN	INSERTION	ACTION	INNERVATION
Levator ani	Posterior surface of pubis, ischial spine	Coccyx	Support pelvic organs. Supports pregnant uterus, participates in childbirth	Pudendal
Coccygeus (posterior continuation of levator ani)	Ischial spine	Coccyx, sacrum	Same as levator ani	Pudendal
Spincter ani externus	Coccyx	Central tendon of perineum	Closes anal canal	Pudendal and S4
Spincter urethrae	Pubic ramus	Central tendon of perineum	Constricts urethra	Pudendal
Ischiocavernosus	Ischial ramus	Corpus cavernosum	Compresses base of penis or clitoris	Pudendal
Transverse perinei	Ischial ramus	Central tendon of perineum	Supports pelvic floor	Pudendal
Bulbospongiosus (male)	Perineum and bulb of penis	Central tendon of perineum	Constricts urethra and erects penis	Pudendal
Bulbospongiosus (female)	Central tendon of perineum	Base of clitoris	Erects clitoris	Pudendal

TABLE 5.20   Muscles of the Vertebral Column: Muscles of Erect Posture

NAME	ORIGIN	INSERTION	ACTION	INNERVATION
NOTE: Muscles of the abdominal wall function as postural muscles.				
Iliopsoas	Postural muscle when femur acts as origin	See MUSCLES LOCATED IN THE ANTERIOR HIP		

ERECTOR SPINAE GROUP
Composed of three muscle groups, each of which has subgroups. The three major groups are the laterally placed **iliocostalis**, the intermediately placed **longissimus**, and the medially placed **spinalis**.

NAME	ORIGIN	INSERTION	ACTION	INNERVATION

Iliocostalis
  Lumborum
  Thoracis
  Cervicis
	Iliac crest and all ribs	Ribs or transverse processes roughly six vertebrae above origin	Extends trunk and neck, maintains erect posture, rotates trunk and neck	Dorsal rami of lumbar, thoracic, and cervical spinal nerves

Longissimus
  Thoracis
  Cervicis
  Capitis
	Transverse processes of thoracic and lumbar vertebrae	Transverse processes roughly twelve vertebrae above origin, some ribs, and mastoid process of temporal bone	Extends trunk and neck, maintains erect posture, rotates trunk and head	Dorsal rami of lumbar, thoracic, and cervical spinal nerves

Spinalis
  Thoracis
  Cervicis
  Capitis
	Spinous processes of upper lumbar and lower thoracic vertebrae	Spinous processes of upper thoracic vertebrae, cervical vertebrae and occipital bone	Extends trunk	Dorsal rami of lumbar and thoracic spinal nerves

Semispinalis	Transverse processes of seventh cervical and thoracic vertebrae	Spinous processes roughly six vertebrae above origin, occipital bone	Extends and rotates vertebral column and head	Dorsal rami of spinal nerves
Multifidus	Pelvic girdle, lumbar vertebrae, transverse processes of thoracic and lower cervical vertebrae	Spinous processes three vertebrae above origin	Extends and rotates trunk	Dorsal rami of lumbar, thoracic, and cervical spinal nerves
Quadratus lumborum	Posterior iliac crest and lower three lumbar vertebrae	Twelfth rib and transverse processes of top four lumbar vertebrae	Lateral flexion of trunk, pelvic extension	T12, L1

TABLE 5.21   Muscles Located in the Lateral Hip

NAME	ORIGIN	INSERTION	ACTION	INNERVATION
Tensor fasciae latae	Anterior iliac crest	Through iliotibial band to lateral tibia	Tenses and abducts thigh	Superior gluteal

TABLE 5.22 — Muscles Located in the Anerior Hip

NAME	ORIGIN	INSERTION	ACTION	INNERVATION
Iliopsoas Two components: Iliacus and psoas	Transverse processes of lumbar vertebrae, iliac fossa	Lesser trochanter of femur and iliopubic junction	Flexes and laterally rotates thigh, also flexes trunk	L1–L3
Rectus femoris	See MUSCLES LOCATED IN ANTERIOR THIGH			

TABLE 5.23 — Muscles Located in the Posterior Hip

NAME	ORIGIN	INSERTION	ACTION	INNERVATION
Gluteus maximus	Posterior iliac crest, sacrum, coccyx	Iliotibial tract and gluteal tuberosity of femur	Extends and rotates thigh laterally	Inferior gluteal
Gluteus medius	Lateral surface of ilium	Greater trochanter of femur	Abducts and rotates thigh medially	Superior gluteal
Gluteus minimus	Lateral surface of ilium	Greater trochanter of femur	Abducts and rotates thigh medially	Superior gluteal
Piriformis	Sacrum	Greater trochanter of femur	Abducts and rotates thigh laterally	S1–S2

TABLE 5.24 — Muscles Located in the Anterior Thigh

NAME	ORIGIN	INSERTION	ACTION	INNERVATION
QUADRICEPS FEMORIS GROUP				
Rectus femoris	Anterior inferior iliac spine	Tibial tuberosity via patellar tendon	Flexes thigh and extends leg	Femoral
Vastus lateralis	Greater trochanter and linea aspera	Same as rectus femoris	Extends leg	Femoral
Vastus medialis	Linea aspera of femur	Same as rectus femoris	Extends leg	Femoral
Vastus intermedius (located immediately posterior to rectus femoris)	Anterior surface of femur	Same as rectus femoris	Extends leg	Femoral

TABLE 5.25 — Muscles Located in the Medial Thigh

NAME	ORIGIN	INSERTION	ACTION	INNERVATION
ADDUCTOR GROUP				
Adductor brevis	Inferior pubic ramus	Linea aspera of femur	Adducts, rotates, and flexes thigh	Obturator
Adductor longus	Pubic crest and symphysis pubis	Linea aspera of femur	Adducts, rotates, and flexes thigh	Obturator
Adductor magnus	Ischial tuberosity, ischiopubic ramus	Linea aspera of femur	Adducts, rotates, and flexes thigh	Obturator
Gracilis	Symphysis pubis and pubic arch	Medial surface of tibia	Flexes leg and adducts thigh	Obturator
Pectineus	Pubic spine and iliopubic junction	Pectineal line of femur (distal to lesser trochanter)	Flexes and adducts thigh, rotates thigh laterally	Femoral

TABLE 5.26 — Muscles Located in the Posterior Thigh

NAME	ORIGIN	INSERTION	ACTION	INNERVATION
HAMSTRING GROUP				
Biceps femoris	Long head: Ischial tuberosity Short head: Linea aspera of femur	Lateral portion of head of fibula, lateral tibial condyle	Flexes leg and extends thigh	Tibial and peroneal
Semitendinosus	Ischial tuberosity	Proximal medial tibia	Flexes leg and extends thigh	Tibial
Semimembranosus	Ischial tuberosity	Medial condyle of tibia	Flexes leg and extends thigh	Tibial

TABLE 5.27   Muscles Located in the Lower Leg

NAME	ORIGIN	INSERTION	ACTION	INNERVATION
Gastrocnemius	Lateral and medial tibial condyles, knee capsule	Calcaneus via Achilles tendon	Plantar flexes foot, flexes leg	Tibial
Soleus	Head of fibula, medial surface of tibia	Calcaneus via Achilles tendon	Plantar flexes foot	Tibial
Plantaris	Linea aspera of femur	Calcaneus via Achilles tendon	Plantar flexes foot, flexes leg	Tibial
Popliteus	Lateral condyle of femur	Posterior tibia	Flexes and medially rotates leg	Tibial
Peroneus brevis	Fibula	Metatarsal 5	Plantar flexes foot	Peroneal
Peroneus longus	Fibula and lateral condyle of tibia	Cuneiform 1; Metatarsal 1	Plantar flexes foot	Peroneal
Flexor hallucis longus	Shaft of fibula	Distal phalanx of great toe	Flexes great toe, plantar flexes foot	Tibial
Flexor digitorum longus	Posterior surface of tibia	Distal phalanges of four lateral toes	Flexes toes, plantar flexes foot	Tibial
Tibialis posterior	Interosseous membrane of tibia and fibula	Several tarsals and metatarsals	Plantar flexes foot	Tibial

NOTE: The tendons of the three preceding flexor muscles pass through the ankle just posterior and inferior to the medial malleolus. From posterior to anterior, the order of these tendons is *T*. posterior, F. *d*igitorum longus, and F. *h*allucis longus, which has led to their being casually referred to as *T*om, *D*ick, and *H*arry.

NAME	ORIGIN	INSERTION	ACTION	INNERVATION
Extensor hallucis longus	Shaft of fibula, interosseous membrane	Distal phalanx of great toe	Extends great toe, dorsiflexes foot	Deep peroneal
Extensor digitorum longus	Lateral tibial condyle, anterior fibular surface	Middle and distal phalanges of four lateral toes	Extends toes, dorsiflexes foot	Deep peroneal
Tibialis anterior	Lateral condyle and body of tibia	First metatarsal and first cuneiform	Dorsiflexes foot	Deep peroneal
Peroneus tertius	Fibula and interosseous membrane	Metatarsal 5	Dorsiflexes and everts foot	Deep peroneal

TABLE 5.28 — The Cranial Nerves

NUMBER AND NAME	EXIT FROM SKULL	FUNCTION
I. Olfactory	Cribriform plate of ethmoid	Sensory: Olfaction. Rhythmic sensitivity follows hormonal cycles in females.
II. Optic	Optic foramen	Sensory: Vision. Probable efferents may regulate retinal metabolism and structural renewal.
III. Oculomotor	Orbital fissure	Motor: Rectus superior, rectus inferior, rectus medius, and obliquus inferior muscles. Sensory: Proprioception. Autonomic (parasympathetic): Muscles of iris, ciliary muscle to control lens.
IV. Trochlear	Orbital fissure	Motor: Obliquus superior muscle. Sensory: Proprioception.
V. Trigeminal		
Ophthalmic branch	Orbital fissure	Sensory: Cornea, upper eyelid, scalp, skin of upper face.
Maxillary branch	Foramen rotundum	Sensory: Palate and upper jaw, teeth and gums, nasopharynx, skin of cheek, lower eyelid, upper lip.
Mandibular branch	Foramen ovale	Sensory: Lower jaw, teeth and gums, anterior two-thirds of tongue, mucous membrane of cheek, skin of lower lip, chin, and ear. Motor: Muscles of chewing, throat, middle ear.
VI. Abducens	Orbital fissure	Motor: Rectus lateralis muscle. Sensory: Proprioception.
VII. Facial	Stylomastoid foramen and internal auditory meatus	Motor: Muscles of facial expression, throat middle ear. Sensory: Proprioception, taste (anterior two-thirds of tongue), palate. Autonomic (parasympathetic): Tear glands, salivary glands, and secretory glands in pharynx.
VIII. Auditory	Internal auditory meatus	Sensory: Hearing (cochlear branch), balance (vestibular branch).
IX. Glossopharyngeal	Jugular foramen	Sensory: Posterior one-third of tongue, posterior pharynx, taste (posterior one-third of tongue), proprioception. Motor: Pharyngeal muscle. Autonomic (parasympathetic): Salivary glands, carotid sinus.
X. Vagus	Jugular foramen	Sensory: Inferior pharynx, larynx, internal organs. Motor: Posterior pharynx, larynx, tongue. Autonomic (parasympathetic): Thoracic and abdominal viscera.
XI. Spinal accessory	Jugular foramen	Motor: Posterior pharynx, sternocleidomastoid, trapezius muscles. Sensory: Proprioception.
XII. Hypoglossal	Hypoglossal canal	Motor: Tongue and throat. Sensory: Proprioception.
XIII. Vomeronasal	Internal to skull	Parts of nasopharynx. May allow desert mammals to sense humidity. Function in humans unknown; may respond to pheromones.

Several mnemonic devices exist to aid remembering the names of the 12 standard cranial nerves in order. The most common (and least bawdy) of these is: "On Old Olympus' Towering Tops, A Finn and German Viewed Some Hops." The recently discovered unpaired thirteenth cranial nerve is not contained in this rhyming couplet.

TABLE 5.29   Spinal Nerves and Their Branches

NERVE	SPINAL COMPONENT		INNERVATION
CERVICAL PLEXUS: C1, C2, C3, C4			
	Superficial cutaneous branches		
	Lesser occipital	C2, C3	Skin of scalp above and behind ear
	Greater auricular	C2, C3	Skin in front of, above, and below ear
	Transverse cervical	C2, C3	Skin of anterior aspect of neck
	Supraclavicular	C3, C4	Skin of upper portion of chest and shoulder
	Deep motor branches		
	Ansa cervicalis		
	Anterior root	C1, C2	Geniohyoid, thyrohyoid, and infrahyoid muscles of neck
	Posterior root	C3, C4	Omohyoid, sternohyoid, and sternothyroid muscles of neck
	Phrenic	C3–C5	Diaphragm
	Segmental branches	C1–C5	Deep muscles of neck (levator scapulae ventralis, trapezius, scalenus, and sternocleidomastoid)
BRACHIAL PLEXUS:C5, C6, C7, C8, T1			
	Axillary	Posterior cord (C5–C6)	Skin of shoulder; shoulder joint, deltoid and teres minor muscles
	Radial	Posterior cord (C5–C8, T1)	Skin of posterior lateral surface of arm, forearm, and hand; posterior muscles of brachium and antebrachium (triceps brachii, supinator, anconeus, brachioradialis, extensor carpi radialis brevis, extensor carpi radialis longus, extensor carpi ulnaris)
	Musculocutaneous	Lateral cord (C5–C7)	Skin of lateral surface of forearm; anterior muscles of brachium (coracobrachialis, biceps brachii, brachialis)
	Ulnar	Medial cord (C8, T1)	Skin of medial third of hand; flexor muscles of anterior forearm (flexor carpi ulnaris, flexor digitorum), medial palm and intrinsic flexor muscles of hand (profundus, third and fourth lumbricales)

T2, T3, T4, T5, T6, T7, T8, T9, T10, T11, T12:

No plexus in these segments; branches run directly to intercostal muscles and skin of thorax.

LUMBOSACRAL PLEXUS: L1, L2, L3, L4, L5, S1, S2, S3, S4, S5

NERVE	SPINAL COMPONENT		INNERVATION
Lumbar	Iliohypogastric	T12–L1	Skin of lower abdomen and buttock; muscles of anterolateral abdominal wall (external abdominal oblique, internal abdominal oblique, transversus abdominis)
	Ilioinguinal	L1	Skin of upper median thigh, scrotum and root of penis in male and labia majora in female; muscles of anterolateral abdominal wall with iliohypogastric nerve
	Genitofemoral	L1, L2	Skin of middle anterior surface of thigh, scrotum in male and labia majora in female; cremaster muscle in male
	Lateral cutaneous femoral	L2, L3	Skin of anterior, lateral, and posterior aspects of thigh
	Femoral	L2–L4	Skin of anterior and medial aspect of thigh and medial aspect of lower extremity and foot; anterior muscles of thigh (iliacus, psoas major, pectineus, rectus femoris, sartorius) and extensor muscles of leg (rectus femoris, vastus lateralis, vastus medialis, vastus intermedius)
	Obturator	L2–L4	Skin of medial aspect of thigh; adductor muscles of lower extremity (external obturator, pectineus, adductor longus, adductor brevis, adductor magnus, gracilis)
	Saphenous	L2–L4	Skin of medial aspect of lower extremity
Sacral	Superior gluteal	L4, L5, S1	Abductor muscles of thigh (gluteus maximus, gluteus medius, tensor fasciae latae)
	Inferior gluteal	L5–S2	Extensor muscle of hip joint (gluteus maximus)
	Nerve to piriformis	S1, S2	Abductor and rotator of thigh (piriformis)
	Nerve to quadratus femoris	L4, L5, S1	Rotators of thigh (gemellus inferior, quadratus femoris)
	Nerve to internal obturator	L5–S2	Rotators of thigh (gemellus superior, internal obturator)
	Perforating cutaneous	S2, S3	Skin over lower medial surface of buttock
	Posterior cutaneous femoral	S1–S3	Skin over lower lateral surface of buttock, anal region, upper posterior surface of thigh, upper aspect of calf, scrotum in male and labia majora in female
	Sciatic	L4–S3	Composed of two nerves (tibial and common fibular); splits into two portions at popliteal fossa; branches from sciatic in thigh region to "hamstring muscles" (biceps femoris, semitendinosus, semimembranosus) and adductor magnus muscle
	Tibial (sural, medial, and lateral plantar)	L4–S3	Skin of posterior surface of leg and sole of foot; muscle innervation includes gastrocnemius, soleus, flexor digitorum longus, flexor hallucis longus, tibialis posterior, popliteus, and intrinsic muscles of the foot
	Common fibular (superficial and deep fibular)	L4–S2	Skin of anterior surface of the leg and dorsum of foot; muscle innervation includes peroneus tertius, peroneus brevis, peroneus longus, tibialis anterior, extensor hallucis longus, extensor digitorum longus, extensor digitorum brevis
	Pudendal	S2–S4	Skin of penis and scrotum in male and skin of clitoris, labia majora, labia minora, and lower vagina in female; muscles of perineum

TABLE 5.30   Cellular Components of Blood

CELL TYPE	DESCRIPTION (WRIGHT'S STAIN)	NORMAL NUMBER (CELLS/μL OF BLOOD)	FUNCTION
Erythrocytes (Red blood cells, RBC)	7.5μ diameter, biconcave disk, no nucleus	4–6 million	Transport of respiratory gases (O_2 and CO_2)
Leukocytes (White blood cells, WBC)		5,000 to 10,000/mm^3	Aid in defense against infections by microorganisms
Granulocytes			
Neutrophil	12–15μ diameter, multilobed nucleus, small pink-purple granules	3,000–7,000 (65% of total leukocytes)	Phagocytosis; elevated in number during acute infections
Eosinophil	10–14μ diameter, bilobed nucleus, large orange granules	100–400 (3% of total leukocytes)	Destroys antigen-antibody complexes, phagocytosizes parasites, involved in allergic response
Basophil	8–12μ diameter, bilobed large purple granules that may obscure nucleus	20–50 (1% of total leukocytes)	Contains biogenic amines; releases heparin, histamine, other chemicals during inflammatory response
Agranulocytes			
Lymphocyte	5–16μ diameter, round or nucleus, indented, single-lobed nucleus, variable amount of cytoplasm	1,500–3,000 (25% of total leukocytes)	Immune response by direct cellular contact or via antibody production; elevated in infectious mononucleosis; suppressed by steroid therapy
Monocyte	12–20μ diameter, horseshoe-shaped nucleus	100–700 (6% of total leukocytes)	Macrophages; phagocytosis
Platelets	2-4μ, appear as cytoplasmic fragments	25,000 to 500,000	Coagulation

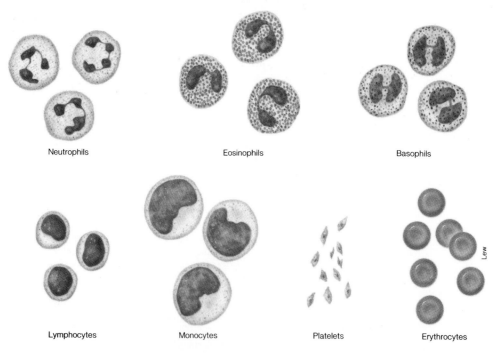

Neutrophils   Eosinophils   Basophils

Lymphocytes   Monocytes   Platelets   Erythrocytes

Figure 5-2
Cellular components in blood.

TABLE 5.31   Events of the Cardiac Cycle

PHASE	ELECTRICAL EVENTS	MECHANICAL EVENTS	HEART SOUND
Late diastole		AV valves open; semilunar valves closed. Blood enters all chambers by passive filling from venae cavae and pulmonary veins.	
Atrial systole	P wave: SA node depolarizes, wave spreads throughout atria P-R interval: Wave of depolarization reaches SA node. Typical P-R interval (beginning of P-wave to onset of next deviation from baseline) is <0.2 seconds	Atria contracted in response to depolarizing signal. Blood engorges ventricles, adding to stretch of ventricular walls.	
Isometric ventricular contraction	QRS complex: Depolarization of SA node. Bundle of His, and Purkinje fibers spread depolarization through valve ring into ventricular muscle	Ventricles contract in response to depolarizing signal. Papillary muscles relax, allowing AV valves to close. Typically, mitral closure slightly precedes tricuspid closure. Reverberation of blood against valve cusps produces low pitched "lub" of first heart sound. With all valves closed, ventricular pressure rises.	First heart sound (may be split with mitral component preceding tricuspid component).
Ventricular ejection	S-T segment: Entire ventricle is uniformly depolarized	Ejection begins when ventricular pressures exceed back pressures in aorta and pulmonary trunk. Semilunar valves open, blood from this cycle enters aorta and pulmonary trunk. Maintained depolarization during S-T segment permits efficient, coordinated ventricular emptying.	
Isometric ventricular relaxation	T-wave	Repolarization wave spreads through ventricles, permitting relaxation. As ventricular pressures drop below those of aorta and pulmonary trunk, semilunar valves close. Typically, aortic semilunar closes slightly before pulmonary semilunar. Reverberation of blood against closed valve cusps creates higher pitched "dub" of second heart sound. Lowered intraventricular pressures permit papillary muscles to pull AV valves open. Ventricular filling begins.	Second heart sound (typically split with pulmonary component slightly following aortic component, especially during inhalation).

TABLE 5.32   Major Blood Vessels and Their Branches

MAJOR ARTERY	MAIN BRANCHES
Ascending aorta	Coronary arteries (right and left)
Aortic arch	Innominate (brachiocephalic) Left subclavian Left common carotid
Innominate	Right subclavian Right common carotid
Common carotid (right and left)	Internal carotid External carotid
Subclavian (right and left)	Vertebral (right and left) Axillary (continuation of subclavian)
Axillary	Brachial (continuation of axillary)
Brachial	Radial Ulnar
Radial and ulnar	Palmar arches (superficial and deep)
Circle of Willis	Vertebrals join in cranium to form basilar artery, which then divides to form left and right posterior cerebral arteries. Internal carotids, upon entering cranium, become left and right anterior cerebral arteries. A pair of posterior communicating arteries and an anterior communicating artery join the cerebrals to form an arterial anastomosis, the circle of Willis.
Descending aorta	Intercostal arteries and spinal branches Celiac trunk (branches to hepatic, splenic, and right and left gastric arteries) Mesenteric (superior and inferior) Renal (right and left) Gonadal (spermatic or ovarian; right and left) Parietal branches to diaphragm, dorsal skin and skeletal muscles, and spinal cord Common iliac (right and left)
Common iliac	Internal iliac (or hypogastric; right and left) External iliac (right and left)
External iliac	Femoral (right and left)
Femoral	Popliteal (right and left)
Popliteal	Tibial (anterior and posterior; right and left)
Tibial	Plantar arches

MAJOR VEIN	COMMENT
UPPER EXTREMITY (RIGHT AND LEFT)	
Palmar arch (superficial and deep)	
Medial cubital	Connects cephalic and basilic
Median antebrachial	Median antebrachial and median cubital flow into basilic
Radial and ulnar	Radial and ulnar flow into brachial
Basilic and brachial	Basilic and brachial flow into axillary
Cephalic	Cephalic and axillary flow into subclavian
Axillary (continuation of brachial)	Cephalic and axillary flow into subclavian
Subclavian (continuation of axillary)	Flows into innominate (brachiocephalic)

TABLE 5.32 — Major Blood Vessels and Their Branches (continued)

MAJOR VEIN	COMMENT
LOWER EXTREMITY (RIGHT AND LEFT)	
Plantar arch	
Dorsal venous arch	
Anterior tibial	Anterior and posterior tibials unite to form popliteal
Posterior tibial	Anterior and posterior tibials unite to form popliteal
Small saphenous	Flows into popliteal
Popliteal	Popliteal and peroneal unite to form femoral
Peroneal	Popliteal and peroneal unite to form femoral
Femoral	Femoral and great saphenous unite to form external iliac
Great saphenous	Femoral and great saphenous unite to form external iliac
External iliac	External and internal iliacs unite to form common iliac
Internal iliac	External and internal iliacs unite to form common iliac
Common iliac	Flows into inferior vena cava
ABDOMEN	
Lumbar (several pairs)	Flows into inferior vena cava and azygous system
Gonadal (spermatic or ovarian; right and left)	Flows directly into inferior vena cava
Renal (right and left)	Flows directly into inferior vena cava
Suprarenal (adrenal; right and left)	Flows directly into inferior vena cava
Hepatic	Flows directly into inferior vena cava
Mesenteric (superior and inferior)	Flows into hepatic portal system
Splenic	Flows into hepatic portal system
Gastroepiploic (right and left)	Flows into hepatic portal system
Hepatic portal	Conveys blood to liver; hepatic vein flows from liver
THORAX	
Left intercostal	Flows into hemiazygos
Hemiazygos	Flows into azygos
Accessory hemiazygos	Flows into azygos
Right intercostal	Flows into azygos
Azygos	Flows into inferior vena cava
Coronary (right and left)	Flows into right atrium of heart
HEAD AND NECK	
Superior sagittal sinus	
Inferior sagittal sinus	Flows into straight sinus
Straight sinus	Flows into transverse sinus
Cavernous	Flows into petrosal sinus
Petrosal sinus (right and left)	Flows into transverse sinuses
Transverse sinuses (right and left)	Flows into sigmoid sinuses

TABLE 5.32 — Major Blood Vessels and Their Branches (continued)

MAJOR VEIN	COMMENT
Sigmoid sinuses (right and left)	Flows into internal jugular vein
Internal jugular	
External jugular	
Vertebral (right and left)	
Innominate (or brachiocephalic; right and left)	Flows into superior vena cava
Superior vena cava	Flows into right atrium of heart

FETAL SYSTEM

Placenta ➤ Umbilical vein ➤ Ductus venosus (bypasses liver) ➤ Inferior vena cava ➤ Right atrium of fetus ➤ Mostly through foramen ovale ➤ Left atrium ➤ Left ventricle ➤ Mostly to fetal head ➤ Return to right atrium ➤ Mostly to right ventricle ➤ Pulmonary trunk ➤ Mostly through ductus arteriosus ➤ Descending aorta ➤ Common iliac arteries ➤ Internal iliac arteries ➤ Umbilical arteries ➤ Placenta

TABLE 5.33   Major Hormones of the Pituitary Gland

HORMONE	CHEMICAL STRUCTURE	TARGET	REGULATION	MAJOR ACTION
ANTERIOR PITUITARY (ADENOHYPOPHYSIS)				
Growth Hormone (GH, Somatotropin)	Protein	General	GH Releasing Hormone from hypothalamus	Enhances protein anabolism, fat catabolism; enhances growth, wound healing, positive nitrogen balance
Prolactin (Prl)	Protein	Breast tissue	Inhibited by dopamine (a prolactin-inhibiting hormone) from hypothalamus	In female, mimics many actions of GH during pregnancy; enhances breast tissue anabolism for lactation
Adrenocorticotropic hormone (ACTH)	Polypeptide	Adrenal cortex	Corticotrophin releasing hormone from hypothalamus	Promotes secretion of glucocorticosteroids by adrenal cortex
Endorphins (several)	Peptide	Central nervous system neurons	Neural activity in hypothalamus in response to stress and probably suckling	Inhibits transmission of pain impulses; enhances feeling of well-being
Thyroid stimulating hormone (TSH)	Glycoprotein	Thyroid gland	Thyroid releasing hormone (TRH) from hypothalamus	Stimulates release of thyroid hormones
Follicle stimulating hormone (FSH)	Glycoprotein	Gonads	Gonadotropin releasing hormone (GnRH) from hypothalamus	Female: Maturation of ovarian follicle; estrogen secretion Male: Sperm production
Luteinizing hormone (LH)	Glycoprotein	Gonads	Gonadotropin releasing hormone (GnRH) from hypothalamus	Female: Rupture of follicle; ovulation Male: Testosterone secretion
POSTERIOR PITUITARY (NEUROHYPOPHYSIS)				
Antidiuretic hormone (ADH, Vasopressin)	Peptide	Kidney tubules	Neural activity in hypothalamus in response to brain osmoreceptors; stress	Increase water retention; elevation of blood pressure
Oxytocin	Peptide	Breast tissue, uterus	Neural activity in hypothalamus in response to suckling, uterine stimulation	Let down of milk in lactating breast; uterine smooth muscle contractions

NOTE: The above-named list of hormones is not an exhaustive list of substances now known to be secreted by the pituitary gland. In addition, the listed hormones are known to have several actions, many of which are also not included.

INDEX